New Rhetorics

EDITED BY

Martin Steinmann, Jr.

UNIVERSITY OF MINNESOTA

CHARLES SCRIBNER'S SONS   *New York*

Foreword

THOUGH it is by no means certain that a new rhetoric has appeared, it is certain that more and more scholars—linguists, psychologists, and philosophers, for example—are contributing to new rhetorics. I say "new rhetorics" rather than "a new rhetoric" because modern concepts of rhetoric are so diverse that a family of new disciplines rather than a single one seems to be evolving. Indeed, "What is rhetoric?" is one of the questions at issue in some of the twelve essays collected here.

But these new disciplines *do* constitute a family, and these diverse concepts of rhetoric *do* bear a family resemblance to one another. Perhaps the resemblance consists in this: that, insofar as rhetoric as a discipline is a linguistic discipline, its object is, in some way or in some sense, *rhetoric as the art of effective expression.* "Rhetoric," in all these concepts, refers at least to both the art of effective expression and the study of that art. Contrasted with *effective* expression, the province of rhetoric, is *correct* expression, the province of syntax, phonology, and semantics.

A game is an illuminating analogy. Every game has two sorts of rule: rules of the game, describing the *correct* moves, and rules of strategy and tactics, describing the *effective* moves. In the language game, the rules of syntax, phonology, and semantics are rules of the game. Players of the language game know these rules and, occasional incorrect moves apart, conform

to them. If they didn't, they simply wouldn't be playing
the game. A game *is* its rules: English *is* the rules of
English syntax, phonology, and semantics. But not
all players of the language game win. Knowing and
conforming to the rules of the game, though a necessary
condition of winning, is obviously not a sufficient condition. In the language game, the rules of rhetoric
are rules of strategy and tactics.

Every rule of rhetoric is, then, a rule of strategy or
tactics; but whether every rule of strategy or tactics
is a rule of rhetoric—whether every linguistic choice
concerning which the rules of syntax, phonology,
and semantics are silent is a rhetorical choice—is another question at issue. Is a choice among arguments
(in classical rhetoric, invention) a rhetorical choice? A
choice among orders of arguments (arrangement)? A
choice among synonymous expressions (style)? Are there,
indeed, any synonymous expressions? Or, what comes
to much the same thing, are form and meaning, form
and content, separable? Are stylistic choices, for instance, really choices among meanings rather than
choices among forms having the same meaning? These
are some of the particular questions at issue.

Because modern concepts of rhetoric are diverse, no
single concept of rhetoric has guided my choice of the
twelve essays collected here; because these concepts do,
however, bear a family resemblance to one another, I
have passed over, often very reluctantly, essays contributing to disciplines clearly outside the rhetorical
family—syntax, semantics, logic, and pedagogy, for
example. (Whether an essay has the term "rhetoric" in
its title is, by the way, no sure test of whether it is about
rhetoric. I. A. Richards' *The Philosophy of Rhetoric*

[1936], for example, is chiefly a contribution to semantics. On the other hand, some of the essays collected here—Stevenson's and Ross's, for example—don't use the term at all.) Though none of these essays is purely or even chiefly historical or encyclopedic, some of them incorporate useful surveys or sketches of rhetoric or parts of rhetoric: Booth's, of modern rhetorical practice; Steinmann's, of some current rhetorical research; Hovland, Janis, and Kelley's, of some sorts of experimental research; Young and Becker's, of classical rhetoric; and Ohmann's, Milic's, and Beardsley's, of diverse concepts of style.

The headnote to each essay, in part biographical, indicates something about its focus, its thesis, and its relationship to some of the other essays.

All texts have been taken from the original editions or are otherwise authoritative.

Martin Steinmann, Jr.

Minneapolis
May 20, 1966

Table of Contents

The Revival of Rhetoric

WAYNE C. BOOTH

Wayne C. Booth (1921-   )—rhetorician, literary critic, and teacher—was born in Utah and educated at Brigham Young University and the University of Chicago, and has taught at Haverford College, Earlham College, and the University of Chicago, where he is now dean of the College. Among his works are many articles on rhetoric and literature and *The Rhetoric of Fiction* (1961). "The Revival of Rhetoric," an address delivered at the annual meeting of the Modern Language Association of America in 1964, states a paradox—that ours is a rhetorical age without a rhetorical theory—and calls for a revival of rhetoric as a discipline—not a revival of old rhetorics but creation of a new rhetoric, a comprehensive theory that will take account of both the pervasiveness and the peculiar character of modern rhetorical practice.

As teachers of language and literature, you have all noticed that my title is even more ambiguous than most. Those of you who are amiably disposed may even have called it general, in the old style, rather than ambiguous, in the new. The word "rhetoric" has for a long time served for both the study of the art of persuasion and for the art itself; Aristotle's *Rhetoric*, upper-case, is still unsurpassed, but take away the capital letter and Aristotle's rhetoric is often very bad indeed, at least as we view it. In the second sense rhetoric has never had a real quantitative revival because it has always thrived; but in the first sense we seem to be in the midst of a revival of rhetoric unmatched in the twentieth century. Unfortunately, in spite of some very good work, there are signs that it may prove a very shoddy revival indeed, with no more lasting effect than the rhetorically-oriented "communications" movement of a decade ago, unless we take thought about what we are doing. Judging from some of the recent freshman texts I have seen, I would not be surprised to find in my box tomorrow when I return a new work entitled *A Speller's Rhetoric*.

What, exactly, are we reviving? As applied to art, the term is today given every conceivable degree of narrowness and generality, meaning anything from mere ornamental figures that can be tacked on a discourse or subtracted at will to the whole range of all possible forms of discourse; as systematic study, rhetoric may be anything from a classification of ornamental figures to the theory of man as a logos-possessing animal. What is worse, one cannot even now, after nearly a decade of revived popularity, predict whether the term will be used to refer to something good or something bad. In

From *PMLA*, LXXX (May, 1965), 8–12. Reprinted by permission of the Modern Language Association and the author from *PMLA*.

publications for freshmen it has recently been an O.K.-
term. Yet it is still used in ways that might well deter
us from calling ourselves "Professors of Rhetoric." Listen
to Malcolm Muggeridge, in a recent *Esquire* article:
"Like a man in a dark place without a lantern, Churchill
in his war memoirs has to fall back on shouting—that is,
rhetoric, which is a factor of power rather than of understanding. If the Sermon on the Mount had been expressed rhetorically it would have made little impact,
and that only at the moment of delivery. . . . Churchill's
rhetoric, like Henry V's in Shakespeare's play, was essential for war purposes, but proves increasingly disastrous
as a literary style."

Here, as in much of current usage, rhetoric is still
bombast, mere propaganda, perhaps necessary for the
affairs of men but necessarily tainted, anti-literary. Now
obviously I did not come here to plead for a revival of
such stuff. But I might well have come to describe how
it feels to live in an age dominated by it. A case could
be made for the claim that we live in the most rhetorical
age of all time, if by rhetoric we mean whatever men do
to change each other's minds without giving good reasons for change. I have in mind not only our fantabulous
annual expenditures on advertising and public relations
and political campaigns, though these alone might brand
us, quantitatively, as the most rhetorical age of all time.
I am thinking even more about how image building and
propaganda have come to dominate fields where traditionally one could expect to find not blandishment or
trickery but either solid action or genuine argument. The
hand that used to guide the plow now pens the Agricul-
tural Association Press Release. The warrior's sword is
now either literally a typewriter or, if still in fact a

destructive weapon, one that is wielded not so much to win battles as to change men's minds. The whole affair in South Viet Nam, as President Johnson has said, is carried on in order to prevent Peking and Hanoi "from *thinking* that their current policy of military force will pay dividends" [my italics]. Our nuclear deterrent power is not discussed much any more in terms of its superior strength—nobody doubts that—but in terms of its "credibility." But surely credibility is a rhetorical term. We ask not whether our weapons will destroy you but whether you *believe* that they will destroy you.

I could go on through almost every part of our lives and show a similar reliance on suasion rather than substance. In journalism we find traditional notions of news accuracy replaced more and more, especially in the news magazines, by standards of rhetorical effectiveness; in place of the facts we are titillated and aroused by weekly collections of little short stories, rhetorically organized to sell an editorial point of view. Or again, our notions of personal worth, once decided by such hard substantive matters as moral virtue, or family history, or money in the bank, are now settled rhetorically. The new annual publication, *Celebrity Register*, as Daniel Boorstin has pointed out, says of itself: "We think we have a better yardstick than the *Social Register*, or *Who's Who*, or any such book. . . . It's impossible to list accurately the success or value of men; but you *can* judge a man as a celebrity—all you have to do is weigh his press clippings." But of course *Who's Who* is not much different. Its criterion is announced under the exalted phrase, "subjectivity of reference," which, after long puzzlement, I take to mean simply the number of times people are likely to want to look you up.

More significant to us here, perhaps, is the transformation of intellectual disciplines to mere rhetorical uses—to continue to think of rhetoric as divorced from genuine argument. I have a strong conviction, difficult to prove, that standards of controversy in history, philosophy, and literary criticism—to name only three—have become less and less substantive throughout this century; irrelevant blandishment, name-calling, sheer one-upmanship have increased, while solid argument has diminished—sometimes to the point of disappearing altogether.[1] There are, of course, splendid exceptions in all disciplines; if there were not, the disciplines would themselves disappear. But I invite you to examine your favorite journal—even

[1] Critical comments by two of my friends have made me think that this claim is not only difficult to prove but quite probably mistaken. Mr. Ronald Crane suggests that it reflects plain ignorance of just how low controversy sank in previous centuries. "Have you read the attacks on Bentley?" Mr. Laurence Lerner reminds me of the standards, if they can be called that, of political controversy in the seventeenth century. And I remind myself, now, of what public debate could be like in nineteenth-century England and America.

Clearly the sweeping historical claims that run throughout this first section of my talk are in no way demonstrated by my examples. They might, in fact, be taken as illustrations of the very thing I am claiming to oppose: the use of mere assertion (the more extreme the better) in place of careful argument. Fortunately my argument that we need more and better rhetorical theorizing does not depend on the extreme claim that we are the *most* rhetorical age: it is enough that our lives are permeated by rhetoric, good or bad, and nobody doubts that.

I still suspect, *pace* Mr. Crane, that we are *quantitatively* the most rhetorical age in history—and not only in the undeniable sense that more men are living by rhetoric than ever before. Surely the *proportion* of rhetorical activities to non-rhetorical (like plowing, shearing, or building) is higher now than ever before. But this modified claim, a radical retreat from my original assertions, may be unimportant, and it is certainly one that would be hard to prove (Crane: "Can you think of any previous age with as much pure science or pure music? These two areas are *less* rhetorical than ever before").

if it is one of those few that have tried to maintain
serious standards—and count the number of solid reasons
offered for conclusions as compared with irrelevant ploys
like built-by-association, old-hatism, and so's-your-old-
thesis-chairman. Wherever one looks one is likely to find,
in place of a coherent effort to move from evidence to
conclusions, an outpouring of what one of my colleagues
calls a mere rhetoric of conclusions. Controversy is conducted as if all strong effects were equally valuable; to
shock or simply to win are more important than the
discovery of truth. I announce no secrets here, of course;
many of our most prominent controversialists have explicitly repudiated reason in the name of rhetorical
effects like shock or outrage.

In short, it is not difficult to find signs that we are a
rhetorical age, if we mean by that—once again—an age
in which men try to change each other's minds without
giving good reasons for change. I know of no past culture where power was so persistently thought of as
power to manipulate men's minds; where beauty was so
persistently tested by mere popularity or salability;
where the truth of propositions was so persistently
judged by whether this or that group accepts them;
where notions of human greatness were so persistently
reduced to the question of fame or "national luminosity";
where, finally, educational goals and methods were so
persistently reduced to the notion of conditioning or
imposition of already formed ideas or practices upon an
infinitely malleable material.

I might very well, then, have come to plead for a
further revival of rhetorical studies in order to protect
ourselves and our students from rhetoric as a bad thing.
Many popular prophets have in fact, like David Riesman

in his portrayal of the other-directed man, implored us
to find a mode of guidance for our lives somewhat more
substantive than a perpetually operating radar set turned
to receive rhetorical directions from other members of
the lonely crowd.

But I have played too long with a definition that I
don't believe in. Rhetoric can mean good things, too. All
of the critics who have taken part in the revival of
rhetorical studies that began in the mid-fifties have
defined the term in ways that would require us to speak
of "*bad* rhetoric" when we refer to the perversions I have
just described. The definition of *good* rhetoric, or of
rhetoric in general, good *and* bad, varies from critic to
critic. But beneath the differences there is general agreement that to engage with one's fellow men in acts of
mutual persuasion, that is, of mutual inquiry, is potentially a noble thing. Indeed, none of the corruptions
found in our rhetorical time would even be possible in
a society which had not also laid itself open to the great
virtues of moral and intellectual suasion when properly
used. Consider once again, for example, my summary
description of our rhetorical age. One can easily translate it, proposition by proposition, into a description of
a kind of utopia. Supposing I could say of our society
the following: I can think of no previous society in
which questions of political power were so persistently
referred to the people for consultation and decision;
where questions of beauty were so often decided not by
arbitrary rules imposed by an elite but by reference to
a genuine capacity of art works to please those who
experience them; where questions of truth were so often
tested by debate rather than settled by decree; where
notions of human greatness were so consistently deter-

mined not by fiat of an hereditary aristocracy or plutocracy but by reference to standards testable on the popular pulse; where, finally, educational goals and methods were tested so constantly against practical experience, and where it was unfailingly assumed that, since all men are educable—that is, subject to good rhetoric—there is no limit to the good that can be done through improving the rhetoric of education. Would not such a society— fully as rhetorical as the earlier one—be a noble thing indeed? All of the evils of a rhetorical age are thus corruptions of tendencies that might be ennobling, or at least liberating. Or, to put it again in terms of Riesman's radar set owned by the other-directed man, everything depends on how the radar set is aimed and on the quality of the messages received. An other-directed society would be an ideal society if the "others" were in fact bearers of truth, goodness, and beauty.

Why is it, then, that so much of what we see about us, so much that is done in the name of advertising, of news reporting, of political campaigning, of education, is so cheap, so obviously aimed at persuasion without justification? If I thought I could get away with it here, I might intone an answer something like this: the bad rhetoric of our rhetorical time can be blamed on our almost total failure to develop good rhetorical theory adequate to our needs. I could not get away with such oversimplification, because you are all aware of how little can be changed, directly, by *any* theory, good or bad. But perhaps I *can* get away with a statement only slightly less forceful: of all the causes of our rhetorical shoddiness, the only one that you and I have much chance of doing anything about is our shoddy rhetorical theory and our shoddier teaching thereof. To our non-majors we have offered a collection of high school and freshman textbooks that, with a few exceptions, are as shameful as any of the ills they purport to cure. To our majors, graduate and undergraduate, we have offered even less: at most universities still a student cannot undertake serious rhetorical study even if he wants to, for lack of teachers, courses, or library facilities.

Finally, what have we offered to the public? That the American public wants rhetorical assistance in an age of rhetoric is shown by the almost incredible success of a popular rhetorician like Rudolf Flesch. Flesch's sophistries about achieving an interesting style by using short words, short sentences, and a personal tone are dangerous, but it is hard to think of what guide to recommend to a literate adult in their place. If someone asks me for works that will help him in reading poetry, I can suggest dozens of respectable works, some of them very good indeed. But if I am asked for guidance in distinguishing good controversial argument from bad, or in constructing a really powerful argument on one's own, or even in constructing an effective—not just a passable—staff report, what do I say? Where, in all of our textbooks about how to write, do we send an intelligent adult for guidance in the true arts of transferring ideas, motives, intentions from his mind to other men's minds?

Please don't try to fob me off with the title of your favorite freshman text. There are some good ones, but we must be quite clear about what is needed, and it is not to be found in works designed, for the most part, for semi-literates. What is needed can be seen clearly if we ask where I might turn, in the available rhetorics, for help in improving this talk. I can get help in improving my diction and sentence structure, help of a general kind, from most freshman texts. But where is the theory, where are the practical rules for ensuring that this talk will not only grab you, as the Madison Avenue rhetoricians say, but keep you grabbed and send you away determined to behave differently?

Most of the rhetorical advice I find, even in texts that go beyond simple formulae for correctness, is entirely general. Be brief. Be clear. Be forceful. Revise carefully. Use short words. Such advice is not plainly wrong. It can even be useful. But since it is general, it gives me no help in deciding what arguments might appeal to you, sitting out there in all your particularity on a particular occasion. What appeals are available to me? What order should I give them? Brevity, clarity, unity, coherence, emphasis—none of these will be worth a brass farthing with you unless somehow I have managed to invent an organized chain of arguments about *this* subject for *this* audience that will bridge the gap between what you believed when you came and what I want you to believe when you depart. But you will look a long while in the available modern rhetorics before you will find much that could possibly help me in this central task.

I do find considerable help about such matters in Aristotle and the many traditional rhetorics fathered by him. They all tell me to look to my arguments and to make sure that there is at least a semblance of genuine connection between them and my conclusions. They all tell me, more importantly, that what will *be* a semblance of sound connection can be decided only by considering my audience, and they all give me, by implication, some notion of what a large gathering of more-or-less-middle-aged and thoroughly fatigued teachers of language and literature will demand or allow, as a ratio of real proof to other, incidental appeals. They all suggest ways of handling emotional appeals and those essential, disguised claims that I am a citizen of good standing in the world of letters. I find it interesting, incidentally, that with all our modern passion for inventing new studies with proper labels we do not even have words in our language for the sciences of invention and arrangement or for the study of emotional and ethical appeal. With all our new grammars and new stylistics, with our proxemics and tagmemics, surely it is time for someone to make himself a professor of inventionics or arrangementistics.

The traditional rhetorics had terms for such matters, and they can still give us more help than most of us suspect. We would be in much better condition if everyone now reviving rhetoric took at least the trouble to learn one traditional rhetoric thoroughly.

But it would be naive to think that reviving Aristotle or Quintilian or Campbell or Whately could solve our problems if we only studied them carefully. For one thing, the age of rhetoric has invented forms of persuasion that earlier ages knew not of. Much, perhaps most, of our rhetoric occurs in informal situations; we need a rhetoric of the symposium, of the conference room—I would hope somewhat more respectable intellectually than what is now offered the public under terms like "group dynamics" and "conference techniques."

Perhaps more important, we cannot take for granted, as most traditional rhetoricians felt that *they* could, a systematic coverage under other categories of such matters as logic and dialectic. Our students are not trained, as they could assume of their students, in the analysis of serious argument. Whether we choose to extend the

term rhetoric to include the whole art of meaningful
discourse or confine it to non-belletristic, obviously persuasive forms, or confine it even further to the paralogical
elements in such persuasive forms, we must find some
place in our revived rhetorical studies for training in how
to build arguments that coerce, by their cogency, the
agreement of all who will attend to them. Traditional
logics and grammars will help us here, but I suspect that
modern logics and semantics and grammars will prove
indispensable. The revival, here again, must do more
than echo the past.

But this leads to a final reason for rejecting the notion
that the revival of rhetoric can mean only the revival of
earlier rhetorics. It is simply that none of them can
possibly give us the comprehensive rhetorical theory we
seek. Living in a new kind of rhetorical age, surrounded
by, indeed practicing daily, forms of persuasion their
authors never dreamed of, we inevitably hunger for a
theory that will do justice to *our* manifold rhetorical
experiences, and we do not find that the categories used
by earlier theorists quite do the job. I can illustrate this
point by asking if you have not felt impatient, so far in
my talk, by my omission of the rhetoric of literature. I
have talked as if the whole problem were that of finding
a theory of rhetoric for the teaching of composition. But
you and I are groping for much more than that, as we
work at reviving this old, magical term. Why have some
of the greatest theorists of our time—men like Richard
McKeon and Kenneth Burke—found themselves trying to
construct unified rhetorical views of all the verbal arts?
Obviously I cannot answer this rhetorical question about
rhetoric in our time, but I can suggest an answer by
asking another: Why do we find ourselves gathered here

engaged in rhetoric about rhetoric and literature? Whatever answer we give must include, I think, a recognition
that we are a rhetorical age in a sense far more profound
than the one I began with. We believe in mutual persuasion as a way of life; we live from conference to conference. More significantly, the intellectual inquiries of our
time, even at their most responsible level, have tended
to be inquiries that can best be called rhetorical. In
philosophy we do not begin with metaphysical questions
and pursue *being* and *substance* to the bitter end; rather,
we begin with existentialist commitment, induced by
rhetorical works in philosophical garb, or we analyze
the uses of language. We *do* philosophy on each other,
as it were, rather than pursue truth as if it were a thing
to be obtained. In literary criticism, similarly, we have
constructed innumerable semantics and rhetorics and
stylistics and linguistics. Even our histories tend to be
histories of linguistic or rhetorical fashion. New sciences
like cybernetics are invented to unite all human inquiry
under one science of information. Even the so-called
hard sciences are discussed in terms of information
theory. Last month a new interdepartmental committee
was formed at Chicago, to supervise information studies
—I assume that they will be studying the rhetoric of
genes, atoms, and computers.

To try to deal with such a profusion of sciences of
communication with traditional theories would be folly.
We hunger, or at least I hunger, for a comprehensive
view of the arts and sciences of man, a view at least as
comprehensive, say, as the two radically different but
equally thoroughgoing views of Plato and Aristotle.
What we have instead is a logomachy, a rhetorical babel
about forms of rhetoric. And the warring factions wage

their battles without generals and without having had their basic infantry training.

It is time now for me to come out from behind that feeble metaphor and make my main plea quite openly. My rhetorical point to a group of rhetoricians is twofold: first, that in a rhetorical age rhetorical studies should have a major, respected place in the training of all teachers at all levels; and secondly, that in such an age, specialization in rhetorical studies of all kinds, narrow and broad, should carry at least as much professional respectability as literary history or as literary criticism in non-rhetorical modes. Whether we restore the old chairs of rhetoric by name or not, chairs like my own Pullman Professorship ought to exist in every department, to provide visible proof that to dirty one's hands in rhetorical studies is not a sure way to professional oblivion.

If I had made such a plea for a genuine revival of advanced rhetorical studies ten years ago, I would have had to base my appeal almost entirely on your sense of duty: "the condition of our writing courses demands that we sacrifice ourselves by doing the unpopular thing." But in 1964 one can indulge in that appeal dear to the hearts of all rhetoricians, namely: "Here for once duty and profit and pleasure are reconciled." The fashionable demand for rhetorical studies is such that even the worst textbook profits from the word rhetoric in the title. (I speak from experience: whatever the faults or merits of *The Rhetoric of Fiction*, it has profited factitiously from my having used a fad term, quite unwittingly, in the title. I learned last month of a teacher who had ordered it as the basic text for his freshman composition course.) If, as I am assuming, you want to do serious intellectual work without undue penalties from society, and if—like most of us—you want your work to have some relevance to the real needs of society, you need neither to blush nor to tighten your belt when you turn from *belles lettres* to rhetoric.

To those of you who feel that your present research is trivial though respected, I would say: drop that study of Phineas Fletcher or of Suckling's imitators and take up the great rhetorical theorists and the great rhetoricians who helped to mold our age. Those of you, on the other hand, who are doing seemingly non-rhetorical literary study that you know to be not in the least trivial can find both fun and profit in discovering what happens if you grasp your subject by a rhetorician's handle. Best of all, you might in the process even discover how to make literary studies genuinely relevant to the literate and semi-literate public of a rhetorical age.

Rhetorical Research[*]

MARTIN STEINMANN, JR.

Martin Steinmann, Jr. (1915-   ), was born in Minnesota and educated at the University of Minnesota, where he is now professor of English. He has published works on literature, criticism, logic, language, and freshman composition. "Rhetorical Research" holds that, insofar as rhetorical choices are verbal, they are choices among synonymous expressions (a view that Ohmann, Milic, and Sledd take of those rhetorical choices that are stylistic); sketches a program of research appropriate to this conception of rhetoric; and further documents Booth's thesis that revival of rhetoric as a discipline is urgently needed.

[*] For valuable criticism of earlier drafts of this essay, I am grateful to my colleagues Professors Harold B. Allen and Donald K. Smith and to Professor Newton Garver, of the University of Buffalo.

PERHAPS in no other century than ours have so much intelligence and indeed genius been devoted to the study of language; certainly in no other has the study of language been considered fundamental to so many disciplines—anthropology, engineering, mathematics, philosophy, and psychology, to mention a few. But the century that has revolutionized grammar and logic, for example, and given us structural linguistics, transformational grammar, symbolic logic, linguistic philosophy, and information theory has left rhetoric almost untouched. Who are the Bloomfields, the Sapirs, the Whorfs, the Frieses, the Pikes, the Tragers, and the Chomskys of rhetoric? The Russells, the Wittgensteins, the Carnaps, the Tarskis, the Feigls, the Ryles, and the Ayers? The Shannons, the Weavers, and the Cherrys? Surely not Wendell and Strunk, not Woolley and Scott; nor, for all their brilliant speculations, Kenneth Burke and I. A. Richards. Though certain sorts of rhetorical research are urgently needed, both to enlarge our understanding of language and to shore the teaching of oral and written composition, and this need is beginning to be recognized—and though "rhetoric" (the word, if not the thing) has in recent years become respectable and even fashionable—most rhetorical research is still either merely nominal or of the least needed sorts.

In this essay, I shall try to define "rhetoric," to outline the sorts of rhetorical research most needed and least needed, and, finally, to briefly describe the present state of rhetorical research. My aim in defining "rhetoric" is not to assign a novel meaning to this hospitably ambiguous word, nor yet to engage in lexicography, but rather

From *College English*, XXVII (January, 1966), 278–285. Reprinted with the permission of the National Council of Teachers of English and the author.

to make explicit and precise what is central to but implicit and vague in the classical notion of rhetoric and in this way to state fairly precisely the conditions necessary for needed research.

I

To say precisely what rhetoric is, I must first distinguish two senses of "knowing" easily confused in discussing any discipline having human behavior as its object and then describe the three things of which one must have knowledge if one is to use a language effectively.

There are two senses of "knowing": knowing *how* and knowing *that*. In the first sense, a person is said to know something (a language, say) if he possesses a certain ability, if he can perform in certain ways (speak the language). He has knowledge because he knows *how* to do something. In the second sense, he is said to know something (a language, say) if he possesses either a theory (of grammar and semantics) explaining exercise of a certain ability (speaking the language) or information about some historically given events (certain utterances). He has knowledge because he knows *that* something is the case. Neither sort of knowledge entails the other (thousands of American four-year-olds know English in the first sense but not in the second, and thousands of American adults know some French in the second sense but not in the first). (Cf. Gilbert Ryle, *The Concept of Mind* [London, 1949], ch. 2; W. N. Francis, "Language and Linguistics in the English Program," *CE*, 26 [1964], 14.)

To use a language effectively—to speak or write English, say—one must have, in the *first* sense, knowledge of three things.

First, to speak or write at all, one must know English; that is, know *how* to choose between English and non-English expressions. To know English is to possess the ability to make one's utterances conform to a set of rules —grammatical (concerned with form) and semantic (concerned with meaning and including the rules of deductive logic)—that decide for a given expression whether it is English. These rules do not uniquely determine one's utterances; they simply restrict his range of choice.

Second, to speak or write effectively, one must know *how* to think effectively; that is, know *how* to choose wisely between things to say, between *non*synonymous expressions.

If expressions differ in form (in sounds or sequences of sounds or in characters or sequences of characters) but not in meaning (a certain sort of relation between form and other things), they are synonymous; if they differ in both form and meaning, nonsynonymous. Every difference in meaning entails a difference in form, but not every difference in form entails a difference in meaning. Meaning is inseparable from form, but several forms may have the same meaning: the height of the Empire State Building is inseparable from the Empire State Building, but other buildings may have the same height.

As Gilbert Ryle has shown (*The Concept of Mind*), to think is to choose between nonsynonymous expressions; thought and expression are inseparable; having a thought and giving it some expression—in English or Turkish, say, or (since not all expressions are utterances) in a diagram—are not distinct, successive activities. One

does not conceive a theory and then express it; he con-
ceives it by expressing it; and, if he cannot express it,
he doesn't have it. One does not solve a jig-saw puzzle
and then express his solution; he solves it by expressing
his solution, by fitting the pieces together correctly or,
at least subvocally, giving an account of how they may
be correctly fitted together; and, if he can't do this, he
doesn't have a solution. A thought too deep for expression is not a thought. (Cf. Kenneth Pike, "A Linguistic
Contribution to Composition: A Hypothesis," *CCC*, 15
[1964], 82-88, esp. 83.) And, of course, not all of one's
responses, verbal or otherwise, are thoughts or expressions of thoughts. Conditioned responses—recitation of
maxims, cocktail-party chatter, selection of the right
gear, or shaking hands—are neither thoughts nor expressions of thoughts. But most utterances are not conditioned responses, for most utterances are unique. Indeed,
this very sentence—"But most utterances are not conditioned responses, for most utterances are unique"—has
probably never been uttered before and, except (as
now) within quotation marks, will probably never be
uttered again. The creativity that produces (and under-
stands) unique utterances, often noted by Noam
Chomsky (e.g., review of Skinner's *Verbal Behavior*,
Language, 35 [1959], 26-58), is the creativity of thought.

Third, to speak or write effectively, one must know
rhetoric; that is, know *how* to choose wisely between
ways of saying the same thing, between synonymous
expressions.

Though thought and expression are inseparable, it
makes sense to say that someone expresses a thought
effectively and to hold that, in saying this, we refer to
three distinct things: (a) a certain person, (b) a certain

thought, and (c) a certain expression of (b). The mistake lies, not in holding this, but in imagining that (b) and (c) are separable—that, for example, (b) is some sort of *event* occurring *within* (a), a thought-thinking that causes (c), say, or of which (c) is a good description or photograph. For every description of this mysterious event turns out to be either identical or synonymous with (c). "(a)," we remark, "certainly expressed his thought effectively when he said, 'Taxation without representation is tyranny.'" But, if we are asked what thought (a) expressed when he said that, we are puzzled by the question and can only reply, "Why, the thought that taxation without representation is tyranny" or "The thought that an un- or disfranchised taxpayer is unfairly put upon." And, if (a) himself is asked this question, he can do no better. The fact is, of course, that, far from being an event occurring *within* (a), (b) is not an event at all, but a relation, and not a relation *within* (a) or even between (a) and something else, but a relation between (c) and something else. In other words, (b) is a meaning—a certain sort of relation between (c), a form, and something else. A thought is a meaning; and it makes sense to say that someone expresses his meaning effectively and to hold that, in saying this, we refer to three distinct things: (a) a certain person, (b) a certain *meaning*, and (c) a certain expression of (b). Meaning is inseparable from form, in the way that cousinage is inseparable from cousins. But, as we have seen, several forms may have the same meaning, several expressions may be synonymous; what is more, some of these synonymous expressions may be *rhetorically* more effective than others.

Rhetoric, then is concerned with the effective choice

of synonymous expressions; but, as the word "effective" suggests, it is concerned, not with utterances only, the mere forms, but with some of their relations to other things. These other things are among the six variables that every act of speech or writing has: the speaker or writer, his utterance, his context (occasion or medium), his audience (listener or reader), his purpose (the effect that he intends his utterance to have upon his audience), and the effect of his utterance upon his audience; and rhetoric is best characterized by reference to these variables.

Rhetorical knowledge in the *first* sense (the knowing-*how* sense) is rhetorical ability—the ability of a speaker or writer to speak or write effectively *insofar as effectiveness can result from (a) his choice of synonymous expressions and (b) his control of those other variables that are within his control.* His choice of *non*synonymous expressions is exercise, not of his rhetorical ability, but of his ability to think; and not all the other variables are within his control. Sometimes, though not always, he can choose his context, his audience, and his purpose; but, obviously, he can never choose to be a different person, another speaker or writer. Granted these qualifications, rhetorical knowledge in the first sense is, then, the ability of a speaker or writer to do such a thing as adapting his utterance to his context, his audience, and his purpose— or adapting his utterance, his context, and his audience to his purpose—and thus producing the response that his purpose calls for.

Rhetorical knowledge in the *second* sense (the knowing-*that* sense) is not an ability (or skill or art) at all, but either a well-confirmed rhetorical theory (explaining either exercise of rhetorical ability or something closely related to it) or a body of rhetorical information (about either historically given utterances or historically given rhetorical theories).

This definition of "rhetoric," though similar to the classical one, is at once broader and narrower. On the one hand, it makes writing as well as speaking (oratory) part of the province of rhetoric; and it does not identify rhetorical effectiveness with successful persuasion but with all successful uses of language. By this definition, successful persuasion is only one sort of rhetorical effectiveness; successful communication of knowledge, for example, is another sort, perhaps the most important. On the other hand, this definition excludes both invention (choosing between nonsynonymous expressions) and memory from the province of rhetoric—retaining arrangement, expression, and delivery (choosing between synonymous expressions)—and it excludes also moral or ethical choices. Central to both definitions, however, is the concept of effective expression: "rhetorice . . . erit bene dicendi scientia" (Quintilian, *Institutio Oratoria* III.iii.12); and, though classical rhetoric embraced much, it emphasized expression, style (e.g., *Institutio* VIII.Pr. 16-17).

II

I shall describe each of five sorts of rhetorical research by indicating its object, its product, and something about its methods of discovery and verification.

Basic rhetorical research investigates exercise of rhetorical knowledge in the *first* sense (the knowing-*how* sense)—that is, exercise of rhetorical ability—and produces rhetorical knowledge in the *second* sense (the

knowing-*that* sense)—specifically, theories of rhetoric
that, to the extent that they are adequate, explain exercise of rhetorical ability. It is basic in the sense that its
object, exercise of rhetorical ability, is the ultimate basis,
the sole *raison d'être*, of every sort of rhetorical research.
Its product, theories of rhetoric, explains this exercise
by rules of rhetoric—rules to which utterances must conform if they are to be counted as effective, rules relating
utterances to the other variables in every act of speech
or writing. Theories of rhetoric are discovered and verified by observation of acts of speech or writing. Ideally,
perhaps, this is observation of experimentally controlled
acts; traditionally, however, it has been either introspec-
tive or absent (intuition).

Basic rhetorical research, experimental or not, must be
distinguished from basic grammatical research, which
investigates exercise of grammatical ability and produces
theories of grammar. Both sorts of research investigate
exercise of abilities that every speaker or writer has; but,
though every speaker or writer of a given language has
equal grammatical ability, not every one has equal
rhetorical ability. Every one, of course, has some rhetorical ability, else his language would be useless to him; but
some have more ability than others. Both sorts of theory,
moreover, explain utterances—and not only historically
given utterances but also those utterances that, though
still unuttered, will, if uttered, be rightly counted as
satisfying a certain criterion; but the criteria are radically different. The criterion of rhetorical effectiveness is
causal; the criterion of grammatical correctness, formal.
The rhetorical effectiveness of an utterance depends
upon its effect; the grammatical correctness, upon its
form. A rhetorical choice is effective if it works; a grammatical choice is correct if it is used.

Metarhetorical research investigates theories of rhetoric (the product of basic rhetorical research) and produces metatheories of rhetoric. If basic rhetorical research is basic in the sense that its object, exercise of rhetorical ability, is the ultimate basis of every sort of rhetorical research, metarhetorical research is basic in the sense that its object, theories of rhetoric, is the basis, a necessary condition, of basic rhetorical research. For metatheories describe (or prescribe) the properties of adequate theories. An adequate metatheory does such things as specifying what an adequate theory must explain (exercise of rhetorical ability) and what methods of discovery and verification it must use and explicating rhetorical concepts like purpose and context. Without metaresearch, there can be no investigation of any phenomenon, exercise of rhetorical ability or any other. The concept of the phoneme, for example, is a product of metagrammatical research (research in structural linguistics); and Chomsky's theory of transformational grammar is a metatheory of grammar. A metatheory of rhetoric, like metatheories generally, is decided upon rather than discovered, is a product of logical analysis rather than of empirical investigation; and it is justified rather than verified—justified to the extent that the theories of rhetoric that conform to it are successful.

These two sorts of rhetorical research are in one sense or another basic, but they are not the only sorts. Indeed, the number of possible sorts is infinite. I shall describe only three other sorts, however—partly because they are the most popular of the other possible sorts, indeed much more popular than basic research and metaresearch, but chiefly because they are often confused with and pass for these two sorts.

Pedagogical rhetorical research investigates exercise

of pedagogical rhetorical ability—the ability to produce rhetorical ability, to teach oral or written composition—and produces theories of teaching rhetorical ability. Its object is not exercise of rhetorical ability (the object of basic research), but one means of acquisition of it, by formal instruction. Theories of teaching rhetorical ability are discovered and verified by observation, not of acts of speech or writing, but of acts of teaching speech or writing.

Rhetorical criticism investigates historically given utterances and produces, not theories, but information about their relationships to exercise of rhetorical ability and to theories of rhetoric. But its object is not this or any other exercise of an ability, and its product not these or any other theories. For a given utterance (Lincoln's Gettysburg address, say, or Dr. Johnson's Preface to his Shakespeare), it shows (not simply recognizes) whether that utterance is a product of exercise of rhetorical ability, or (what comes to the same thing) whether it conforms to the rules of some theory of rhetoric. Information of this sort is discovered and verified by analysis of utterances according to these rules.

Historical or comparative rhetorical research investigates historically given theories of rhetoric and produces information about them and their relationships to one another—either historical (diachronic) or comparative (synchronic). Like rhetorical criticism, it neither investigates exercise of an ability nor produces theories. For a given set of theories of rhetoric (Plato's and Aristotle's, say, or Burke's and Richards'), it shows such things as how the theories resemble and differ from one another and whether one theory seems to have foreshadowed or influenced another.

III

A paradox of rhetorical research is that, though any sort of rhetorical research that does not presuppose much sound basic research and, hence, much sound meta-research is either worthless (like fire-fighting research based upon the phlogiston theory) or merely curious (like historical research into alchemists' quest for the philosophers' stone), our century has preferred pedagogical research, criticism, and historical or comparative research to basic research and metaresearch. And nearly all basic research has been unsound for one or more of a variety of reasons: it has not had the cooperation of competent linguists, logicians, and psychologists; it has been content with discovering and verifying theories by introspection and intuition; it has been given over to propaganda ministries and Madison Avenue, whose severely practical research is unimportant, not because it is practical, but because, yielding few or no generalizations, it is theoretically uninteresting; it has been one-sided, passing off formal or semantic descriptions of utterances as products of basic research—in a word, it has had little sound metaresearch to support it.

There has, of course, been some promising basic research and metaresearch; but, spread out among more than a half dozen isolated disciplines (education, journalism, composition, linguistics, literary criticism, speech, and psychology), it has not come to much. Worth mention are Rudolf Flesch's readability formula (*The Art of Readable Writing* [New York, 1949]); some content analysis (*Trends in Content Analysis*, ed. Ithiel de Sola Pool [New York, 1959]); Francis Christensen's careful analysis of historically given sentences (e.g., "A

Generative Rhetoric of the Sentence," *CCC*, 14 [1963],
155-161) and paragraphs ("A Generative Rhetoric of the
Paragraph," *CCC*, 16 [1965], 144-156) and Zellig S.
Harris' formal analysis of utterances longer than sentences ("Discourse Analysis," *Language*, 28 [1952],
1-30), not in themselves basic research but a good
foundation for it; Robert Graves and Alan Hodge's
excellent *Reader over Your Shoulder* (London, 1943);
literary criticism emphasizing literary conventions, the
author's rhetorical strategies, and the reader's expectations (Burke's; E. E. Stoll's; A. J. A. Waldock's *Paradise
Lost and Its Critics* [Cambridge, Eng., 1947]; Martin
Steinmann, Jr.'s "The Old Novel and the New," in *From
Jane Austen to Joseph Conrad*, ed. Robert C. Rathburn
and Steinmann [Minneapolis, 1958], pp. 286-306; and
Wayne C. Booth's *The Rhetoric of Fiction* [Chicago,
1961]), which, committing the Affective Fallacy, have
had the weight of the New Criticism against them; some
basic experimental research in speech (e.g., Raymond
Smith, "An Experimental Study of the Effects of Speech
Organization upon Attitudes of College Students," *SM*,
18 [1951], 292-301; Kenneth C. Beighley, "An Experimental Study of Four Speech Variables on Listener
Comprehension," *SM*, 19 [1952], 249-258); and the basic
experimental research of the social psychologists associated with the Yale Communication Research Center
(Carl I. Hovland *et al.*, *Communication and Persuasion*
[New Haven, 1953]; *The Order of Presentation in Persuasion* [New Haven, 1957]). But basic research and
metaresearch have come to so little that John B. Carroll's
comprehensive survey, *The Study of Language: A Survey of Linguistics and Related Disciplines in America*
(Cambridge, Mass., 1953), refers to none, though it uses

the word "rhetoric" once, in a section on speech education (p. 158), and mentions the rhetorical level of communication theory: Level C, as yet programmatic (p. 197).

Most surprising is the neglect of basic research and metaresearch by teachers and scholars in English. Few of them, of course, take any interest in language or composition. But most of those who do have long acknowledged the relevance of basic grammatical research and metagrammatical research to the teaching of grammar and composition and the priority of that research to pedagogical grammatical research. Few of them, however, have acknowledged the relevance of basic rhetorical research and metarhetorical research to the teaching of composition and the priority of that research to pedagogical rhetorical research—the favorite nonliterary research of scholars in English being in the grading of themes.

A few examples will suffice to make this point. *Research in Written Composition* (NCTE, 1963), by Richard Braddock *et al.*, concludes "that almost nothing has been proved in a scientific sense about the rhetorical aspects of written composition" (p. 38) and can cite only one piece of basic experimental rhetorical research: John P. Parker, "Some Organizational Variables and Their Effect upon Comprehension," *Journal of Communication*, 12 (1962), 27-32. Albert R. Kitzhaber's *Themes, Theories, and Therapy* (New York, 1963), the most trenchant survey of college composition ever published, says little about rhetoric and nothing about basic research or metaresearch. *The Education of Teachers of English* (New York, 1963), prepared by the NCTE Commission on the English Curriculum and edited by Alfred

H. Grommon, mentions rhetoric only twice (pp. 527, 554-555). Much the same may be said of *Needed Research in the Teaching of English* (Washington, 1963), proceedings of a Project English research conference (May 5-7, 1962) prepared by Erwin R. Steinberg. That so intelligent and well-informed a teacher as Hans P. Guth, in a book that "aims at a unified view of the discipline of English in its current state" (*English Today and Tomorrow* [Englewood Cliffs, N.J., 1964], p. v), can say—either truly or falsely, it makes no difference—that Cleanth Brooks and Robert Penn Warren's *Modern Rhetoric* is "the most authoritative modern rhetoric" (p. 208) is further testimony to the low state of basic research and metaresearch. The most recent relevant work—*Freedom and Discipline in English: Report of the Commission on English* [of the College Entrance Examination Board] (New York, 1965)—holds that an antique theory of English grammar and, more recently, ignorance of structural linguistics and transformational grammar have prevented good grammar-teaching in secondary schools (pp. 18-22); and it recommends that "study in rhetoric and composition above the level of the freshman course" be required for certification to teach secondary-school English (p. 10). But it seems to see no need for basic rhetorical research and metarhetorical research.

Somewhat encouragingly, teachers and scholars in English are beginning to take an interest in rhetoric. "We need urgently to have more scholars turn their attention to rhetorical theory," Kitzhaber says, "so that in the next decade we can bring our knowledge of this discipline abreast of our knowledge of literary criticism and linguistic analysis" ("Reform in English," *CE*, 26

[1965], 342). "In a rhetorical age rhetorical studies should have a major, respected place in the training of all teachers at all levels," Booth says; "and . . . in such an age, specialization in rhetorical studies of all kinds, narrow and broad, should carry at least as much professional respectability as literary history or as literary criticism in nonrhetorical modes" ("The Revival of Rhetoric," *PMLA*, 80 [1965], 12). Articles calling for either a new rhetoric or a revival of classical rhetoric, workshops on rhetoric, textbooks on rhetoric—rhetoric is, as Booth adds, fashionable. I fear that, like English teachers' earlier interests in semantics and structural linguistics and their current interest in transformational grammar, this interest may be only that.

Certainly there is, as Kitzhaber and Booth suggest, an urgent need for serious interest in basic rhetorical research and metarhetorical research. *Freedom and Discipline in English*, Richard Pearson says in the Foreword, "should be viewed as a part of the curricular reform that began in the early 1950's and has swept over the schools . . . and take its place with comparable reports in other subjects, particularly in mathematics, the sciences, and foreign languages" (p. vii). But this report is comparable only insofar as it pertains to teaching language (grammar) and, perhaps, literature. For the teaching of composition, unlike the teaching of these other subjects, has little basic research or metaresearch to support it; of the most relevant sorts, basic rhetorical research and metarhetorical research, it has almost none. Until it does, little can be done to solve its pedagogical problems, not to mention its social, economic, and political ones (see Steinmann, "Freshman English in America," *Universities Quarterly*, 19 [1965], 391-395;

"Freshman English: A Hypothesis and a Proposal," *Journal of Higher Education*, 37 [1966], 24-32). What I fail to find is much evidence that the need for basic rhetorical research is recognized, let alone that such research is underway. As Richard Ohmann says, ". . . rhetoricians have lately taken to using the phrase 'new rhetoric' as if it had a reference like that of the word 'horse,' rather than that of the word 'hippogriff.' I am not at all sure that the wings have done more than sprout" ("In Lieu of a New Rhetoric," *CE*, 26 [1964], 17).

Introduction to *Communication and Persuasion: Psychological Studies of Opinion Change*

CARL I. HOVLAND, IRVING L. JANIS, AND HAROLD H. KELLEY

Carl I. Hovland (1912-1961), Irving L. Janis (1918-   ), and Harold H. Kelley (1921-   ) were all at one time or another associated with the Yale Communication Research Center. Hovland was born in Illinois and educated at Northwestern and Yale Universities, and taught at Yale, where, from 1947 until his death, he was Sterling professor of psychology. Janis was born in New York and educated at the University of Chicago and Columbia University, and since 1947 has taught at Yale, where he is now professor of psychology. Kelley was born in Idaho and educated at the University of California (Berkeley) and the Massachusetts Institute of Technology, and has taught or directed psychological research at the University of Michigan, Yale, and the Universities of Minnesota and California (Los Angeles), where he is now professor of psychology. Hovland, Janis, and Kelley's essay—the Introduction to a report of rhetorical research at the Yale Communication Research Center, *Communication and Persuasion* (1953)—states the focus, the purpose, the principles, and the methods of their research. The focus, like the focus of classical rhetoric, is persuasion; and, consequently, the purpose is to understand "the ways in which words and symbols influence people." But the principles and the methods are those of modern individual and social psychology. Their research tries to take account, not just of the communication itself, its content and organization, but of the other variables in the act of communication: the character of the communicator, the character of his audience, and the responses of his audience, for example. And their method is to test rhetorical hypotheses by means of controlled analytical experiments. Another report of their research is *The Order of Presentation in Persuasion* (1957).

DURING recent years the study of the effectiveness of communication has become a subject of major interest in human relations research. In part this may be ascribed to the important role of mass communications in the economic, political, and social organizations of modern society. The growing interdependence of ever larger numbers of people along with advances in the techniques of transmitting communication have led to a high degree of reliance upon mass media to convey information to various types of public and thereby mold their convictions. Executives in many organizations feel the need to improve their communication systems in order to achieve widespread acceptance of the standards and values necessary to the success of their enterprises. In the sphere of international relations, numerous practical communication problems are posed by the "cold war," particularly for government policy makers who wish to increase our "influence" on the people of foreign countries and to counteract potentially disruptive foreign propaganda. Also, a major concern of agencies such as UNESCO is in developing mass educational programs that will be effective in breaking down psychological barriers which prevent mutual understanding between nations. A similar need has long been apparent to leaders within our own country who have worked to counteract racial, ethnic, and religious prejudices interfering with the consistent operation of democratic values.

All of these problems converge upon the area of scientific inquiry concerned with understanding the ways in which words and symbols influence people. Research in this area is of great practical importance

From *Communication and Persuasion: Psychological Studies of Opinion Change* (New Haven: Yale University Press, 1953), pp. 1-18. Reprinted by permission of Yale University Press.

not only to those who make use of mass media but also to specialists in human relations who rely upon such face-to-face situations as small group conferences or psychotherapeutic interviews. Ultimately, an increase in scientific knowledge in this field may be expected to have even broader social application, affecting preventative psychiatry, child rearing, and education in its broadest aspects.

While research on communication and persuasion is of considerable practical concern, perhaps its greatest attraction for the scientist is that it involves central theoretical problems in individual and social psychology. Study of the way in which opinions and beliefs are affected by communication symbols provides an excellent means for examining the role of the higher mental processes in assimilating the numerous and often contradictory influences impinging upon the individual in everyday life.

To explore this area, a program of coordinated systematic research on variables determining the effects of persuasive communication was begun by the writers several years ago, designated the Yale Communication Research Program. The present volume is a report of this research, delineating the major problems which have been explored, summarizing experiments which have been completed, and discussing the theoretical formulations developed in the course of the work. It is, in a sense, a progress report on the preliminary phases of a long-term research program to investigate the principles involved in persuasive communication.

THE COMMUNICATION RESEARCH PROGRAM

The program may best be described in terms of three of its principal characteristics. The first, already implied, is that it is primarily concerned with theoretical issues and basic research. It is thus to be contrasted with the greater part of research in this area which is of an applied or "action oriented" nature. Practical problems are investigated only to the extent that there is clear indication they will contribute to the formulation of important theoretical issues. It is to be expected, however, that theoretically oriented research will ultimately provide the answers to practical problems, whether it be increasing the effectiveness of persuasive communications or educating the public to resist specious propaganda. As Kurt Lewin once said: "Nothing is so practical as a good theory."

A second characteristic of the research program is that it draws upon theoretical developments from diverse sources, both within psychology and in related fields. It is clear that the problems of communication and opinion change cut across the various scientific disciplines as currently defined. Thus while the primary emphasis of the present program is on a psychological analysis of social influence, hypotheses are derived from several other social science areas. The fact that our hypotheses are derived from diverse theoretical systems makes it, of course, very difficult to develop a single, comprehensive treatment. It is hoped that more intensive work over the next decades will help to reduce the gaps between the various formulations and to integrate the contributions of anthropology, sociology, political science, psychiatry, and psychology into a general theory of communication.

One theory most useful to our work has been the "learning theory" developed by Hull [5] and subsequently adapted to complex forms of social behavior by Miller and Dollard [9], Mowrer [10], and others. The implications of this formulation for responses to symbols are particularly relevant to the study of communication.

For an analysis of the role of learning in the changing of opinions through communication the problem of motivation is of central importance. The motives with which the communication specialists will deal are generally learned, or acquired, motives. In considering these, the hypotheses of Freud and other psychoanalysts are of considerable relevance, and are accordingly drawn upon in analyzing the influence of symbols upon an individual's motivational state.

Another source of theoretical concepts comes from research on the effects of group membership. In considering the factors influencing acquired motivations, one immediately sees that some of the major sources of gratification are to be found in the groups to which the individual belongs. The theoretical formulations of Lewin [7] and his co-workers (e.g., Festinger [2]) have been especially fruitful in analysis of the factors affecting the extent to which membership in groups serves to maintain opinions and attitudes of members, in the presence of powerful pressures to change. Similarly, the concept of "reference group" and the attendant theoretical developments of Sherif [12], Newcomb [11], and Merton and Kitt [8] have provided some provocative leads as to the effects of group awareness and group affiliation.

A final characteristic of the research program lies in its emphasis upon testing propositions by controlled experiment. In the majority of the studies reported the results are obtained from experimental designs in which specially constructed communications are presented under conditions where the effects of the various factors influencing opinion change can be isolated.

The data obtained in the present research program supplement those derived from other researches in this area, which typically base their generalizations on survey and correlational methods. Sometimes the relationships derived from comparing the opinion questionnaire responses of various subgroups shed considerable light on causal factors, but frequently it is impossible to draw valid inferences from such data. An example of the difficulty involved in deriving adequate generalizations from correlational data is provided by the research showing a high correlation between amount of information concerning an ethnic or national group and a favorable attitude toward the group. This result is sometimes interpreted to mean that there is a dynamic relationship between the two variables, and that increasing an individual's information about a group will also tend to make his attitude toward the group more favorable. But the crucial test of this implied cause-and-effect relationship is to determine whether or not the transmission of information actually does change attitudes. To carry out such a test requires a controlled analytical experiment in which the independent factor (amount of information communicated) is varied and the dependent factor (amount of attitude change) is assessed. When studies of this type have been carried out it has been found that the generalization does not necessarily hold [4].

Controlled analytical experiments differ not only from static correlational studies but also from evaluative

studies which employ experimental techniques, where
the only interest is in ascertaining whether or not a
particular communication has an effect. Much of the
research during the 1920's and 30's was of this type.
Studies were designed to determine whether or not mass
communications had any effect at all upon attitude or
else to compare the relative merits of two particular
communications, each differing from the other in numerous respects. This type of research sometimes has practical value, but provides little insight into the causal
factors responsible for differences in the effectiveness of
communications. During recent years there has been
increased emphasis on the isolation of basic factors
related to general theoretical formulations. The present
research program represents a continuation of this approach. In most of the studies an attempt has been made
to devise controlled experiments which vary systematically the basic factors derived from theoretical analysis.

Mainly because of the greater possibility of rigorous
experimental control, the communications employed in
most of the present studies are of the one-way variety:
a fixed communication is presented to a "captive" audience and interaction among the recipients of the communication is restricted. It is the belief of the authors,
however, that most of the basic principles derived from
studying one-way communications will prove applicable
also to the type of persuasion involved in group discussions and in psychotherapy, even though additional
propositions concerning face-to-face interaction effects
will also be required.

It is presumptuous, of course, to expect all problems
to be amenable to investigation in this fashion. Nor can
all propositions concerning communication and opinion

change be submitted to experimental test at the present time. Extensive case-study analysis and opinion surveys are sometimes essential to define an issue more sharply or to ascertain whether the conditions which are theorectically required for a particular outcome are actually present. Moreover, in studying such factors as personality predispositions, which do not lend themselves readily to experimental manipulation, only the nature of the communication can be experimentally controlled.

Even when a controlled analytical experiment shows a given factor to be significantly related to communication effectiveness, the question still remains as to the generality of the relationship. For example, experimental results may show that a communication designed to induce people to volunteer for civilian defense activities is more effective when fear-arousing appeals precede rather than follow the action recommendation. Would the outcome be the same in the case of a different topic? Or a different type of communicator? Or another medium? Or a different type of audience? Or a different type of recommended action? The solution to these problems lies, of course, in replication with strategic variations. The first experiment to test a general hypothesis is capable only of showing that the hypothesis holds true under the conditions represented in the experiment. It is necessary to carry out further investigations of the same hypothesis under carefully selected conditions, assigning different values to the supposedly irrelevant factors. Only in this way can one ultimately determine whether or not the hypothesis is a valid generalization and, if so, whether it requires specification of limiting conditions. Experiments of the type reported in the present volume usually provide only tentative generali-

zations which will have to be tested through later verification and replication.

In this volume we shall not attempt to present a
systematic theory of persuasive communication. Nevertheless, in order to understand our choice of variables
for study and our interpretations of the results, the
reader may find it helpful to know the general framework within which the research was conducted and the
working definitions which were found most useful.
Accordingly a brief discussion of the authors' point of
view concerning the nature of opinion change and the
types of variables involved in persuasive communication
will be presented.

Nature of Opinion Change

"Opinion" will be used in a very general sense to
describe interpretations, expectations, and evaluations—
such as beliefs about the intentions of other people,
anticipations concerning future events, and appraisals
of the rewarding or punishing consequences of alternative courses of action. Operationally speaking, *opinions
are viewed as verbal "answers" that an individual gives
in response to stimulus situations in which some general
"question" is raised.* Consider, for example, a person's
opinion concerning the imminence of another world war.
We would say that an individual has a consistent opinion
on this issue if in general he gives the same answer
whenever the pertinent question is raised. The stimulus
situations in which the question is posed may be extremely varied. Sometimes the individual is asked

directly to tell what he thinks about the issue, perhaps at a formal group meeting or in an informal discussion with a friend. At other times the individual may pose the question to himself, if, for example, he is faced with the problem of deciding whether or not to join a military reserve organization.

The foregoing working definition makes it necessary to comment on the differentiations between "opinion" and "fact" and between "opinion" and "attitude." Both facts and opinions represent "answers" to "questions," and as Hovland, Lumsdaine, and Sheffield [4] point out, it is impossible to draw a sharp distinction between the two. But at one end of a continuum are statements typically regarded as matters of opinion, which are difficult to verify—for example, inferences as to the motives of political leaders, the causes of inflation, or predictions concerning future inventions. At the opposite end are statements which are universally regarded as "incontrovertible" facts. Ordinarily when we speak of persuasive communications we are referring to those which deal with issues that cannot be resolved by direct observation and which present conclusions about which there are differences of opinion.

Both "opinion" and "attitude" refer to implicit responses, and, in theoretical terms, are intervening variables. The relationship between the two is an intimate one. But while the term "opinion" will be used to designate a broad class of anticipations and expectations, the term "attitude" will be used exclusively for those implicit responses which are oriented toward approaching or avoiding a given object, person, group, or symbol. This may be interpreted as meaning that attitudes possess "drive value" (Doob [1]). Another distinguishing factor is the extent to which the two can be verbalized. Opinions are considered to be verbalizable, while attitudes are sometimes "unconscious," e.g., avoidance tendencies mediated by nonverbal processes, such as those involved in conditioned fear.

An important implication of this view is that there will be a high degree of mutual interaction between attitudes and opinions. Changes in general approach and avoidance orientations ("attitudes") may affect one's expectations ("opinions") on a number of related issues. Conversely, and of greater importance for our purpose, changes in opinion may modify one's general attitudes. On one hand, a change in an individual's general attitude of hatred toward a political figure may affect his opinion concerning the man's motives. On the other hand, a change in opinion about the politician's motives may change one's attitude of opposition toward him. Our assumption is that there are many attitudes which are mediated by verbal beliefs, expectations, and judgments and that one of the main ways in which communications give rise to changes in attitudes is by changing such verbal responses.

When we say that opinions are "verbalizable" and are "implicit responses" we mean that they are verbal "answers" that one covertly expresses to himself in inner speech. They are thus distinguishable from *overt* verbal responses, which are the answers expressed to others when the question is accompanied by additional stimuli which either demand or instigate verbalization of the answer. Typically the overt and covert responses are identical. But it sometimes happens, of course, that a person will think one answer to himself and give a different answer to others. In such instances the overt verbalizations would be regarded as inadequate indicators of his opinion—it would be said that he is "dissimulating," "distorting," or "lying." If one accepts this usage, the term "opinion" is then restricted to implicit verbal responses. This would seem a useful definition of opinion since overt responses are apt to vary with the external constraints that are present at the moment when an overt response is demanded, whereas implicit responses may be more consistent. Furthermore, implicit responses will affect the individual's decisions, appraisals, and actions whenever the external constraints are not present. Correspondingly, "opinion change" is defined in terms of a change in the *implicit* verbal response. If, for example, an individual should merely change his overt response while the inner one remains unmodified, we would not call this a change in opinion but would say rather that the individual had learned to conceal or to avoid expressing his true opinion.

The above discussion of opinion change immediately raises an important methodological problem: how can one observe changes in implicit verbal responses? Actually, in order to investigate implicit verbal responses, it is necessary to elicit overt verbal responses. The assumption is made that under certain conditions overt verbalizations will be approximately the same as implicit verbal responses; the methodological problem is to set up these conditions. Various techniques are commonly employed for this purpose. In the case of those opinions which involve shame, guilt, or other disturbances that would motivate conscious or unconscious distortion (e.g., preferences relating to perverse sexual practices or hostile evaluations of authority figures) special interview techniques are necessary, such as those used in psychoanalysis, in which the individual learns to give free associations in a permissive interpersonal setting. With opinions which are usually expressed more freely, less complicated techniques are used. Here, opinion questionnaires, designed and administered in such a fashion as to minimize the tendency to suppress or distort, are frequently employed.

In the experiments on persuasion reported in this volume, the topics typically have been chosen to arouse little motivation for either suppression or distortion. In order further to minimize such tendencies standard methodological precautions have been taken: careful attention has been given to question wording, test administrators are clearly designated as research workers who are dissociated from persons having authority over the respondents, subjects are informed that differences of opinion are to be expected, and usually assurances are given that answers will remain anonymous. Under these conditions, it seems fairly safe to assume that the individual's overt verbal responses will correspond fairly well to his implicit verbal responses.

A related methodological problem arises in connection with the "significance" or generality of an observed opinion change: will the individual respond differently to stimuli other than the specific symbols used in the questionnaire? Will responses other than those required in answering the questionnaire be affected? These questions are often raised indirectly in the form of the more general query: how does one know that the observed change represents a *real* change in *opinion* (and not just a change in response to a questionnaire item)? This problem is one for which satisfactory solutions are difficult to obtain and further methodological investigation is required. Nevertheless, for present research purposes an attempt is made to meet the need for assessing the degree of generality by using a series of questionnaire items which consider the same general issue from a variety of points of view, and by selecting questions involving patterns of verbal stimuli most similar to those found in everyday situations. As a supplement to check-list measures of opinion, free answer questions are some-times included so that the respondent's own phrasing may be used as a check on the generality of response.

Ultimately, of course, the justification for the use of questionnaire methods derives from their utility in en-abling the investigator to observe consistent relationships between communication stimuli and changes in verbal response. The interpretations of these relationships and the generality of the hypotheses which they support can be validated in part by their compatibility with observa-tions from other sources, including intensive interviews of individuals exposed to psychotherapy or to mass com-munications, and behavioral data such as those derived from studies of buying, contributing, and voting.

Nature of Persuasive Communication

We assume that opinions, like other habits, will tend to persist unless the individual undergoes some new learning experiences. Exposure to a persuasive communi-cation which successfully induces the individual to accept a new opinion constitutes a learning experience in which a new verbal habit is acquired. That is to say, when presented with a given question, the individual now thinks of and prefers the new answer suggested by the communication to the old one held prior to exposure to the communication.

What are the factors in the communication situation responsible for this change and how do they operate so as to replace the original verbal response by a new one? Without attempting to give a full theoretical account of this learning process, we shall present a tentative summary of the main factors in communication situations which are assumed to be responsible for producing opinion changes.

One key element in the persuasion situation is, of course, the "recommended opinion" presented in the communication. This element may be conceptualized as a compound stimulus which raises the critical question and gives a new answer. For example, imagine the communicator's conclusion to be that "It will be at least ten years before the United States will engage in a war with Russia." We assume that in presenting this idea the communication contains words which operate as effective stimuli in posing the question, "How long before the United States will be at war with Russia?" At the same time the conclusion states a specific answer, "At least ten years." In the course of a lengthy communication this conclusion may be asserted dozens of times or perhaps only once. Even when a communicator does not give an explicit statement of his conclusion, the indirect verbal statements he presents must operate implicitly to pose a question and suggest an answer; otherwise we would not regard the communication as capable of inducing a new opinion.

When exposed to the recommended opinion, a member of the audience is assumed to react with at least two distinct responses. He thinks of his own answer to the question, and also of the answer suggested by the communicator. The first response results from the previously established verbal habit constituting the individual's original opinion; the second response is assumed to result from a general aspect of verbal behavior, namely, the acquired tendency to repeat to oneself communications to which one is attending. Hence, a major effect of persuasive communication lies in stimulating the individual to think both of his initial opinion and of the new opinion recommended in the communication.

Merely thinking about the new opinion along with the old would not, in itself, lead to opinion change. The individual could *memorize* the content of the conclusion while his opinion remained unchanged. Practice, which is so important for memorizing verbal material in educational or training situations, is not sufficient for bringing about the *acceptance* of a new opinion. We assume that acceptance is contingent upon *incentives*, and that in order to change an opinion it is necessary to create a greater incentive for making the new implicit response than for making the old one. A major basis for acceptance of a given opinion is provided by arguments or reasons which, according to the individual's own thinking habits, constitute "rational" or "logical" support for the conclusions. In addition to supporting reasons, there are likely to be other special incentives involving anticipated rewards and punishments which motivate the individual to accept or reject a given opinion. Discussion of the nature of these incentives will be postponed until later chapters.

It is assumed that there are three main classes of stimuli present in the communication situation which are capable of producing the shifts in incentive described above. One set of stimuli has to do with the observable characteristics of the perceived source of the communication. Another involves the setting in which the person is exposed to the communication, including, for example, the way in which other members of the audience respond during the presentation. Communication stimuli also include important content elements, referred to as "arguments" and "appeals." Whether or not stimuli of these various types operate successfully as incentives depends upon the predispositions of the individual. A successful communication is one in which these various stimuli are both adapted to the level of verbal skill of the individual and capable of stimulating his motives so as to foster acceptance of the recommended opinion.

ORGANIZATION OF THE VOLUME

From the foregoing discussion of opinion and opinion change the reader may be able to predict the topics discussed in this volume. Implicit throughout has been a definition of communication which may be more formally stated as the process by which an individual (the communicator) transmits stimuli (usually verbal) to modify the behavior of other individuals (the audience). This definition specifies the research task as consisting in the analysis of four factors: 1) the *communicator* who transmits the communication; 2) the *stimuli* transmitted by the communicator; 3) the *audience* responding to the communication; 4) the *responses* made by the audience to the communication [3]. These topics parallel closely the well-known formula of *who* says *what* to *whom* with *what effect* [13].

In the subsequent chapters of this book selected topics within each of the four categories will be considered. The topics covered are those for which results are available from studies done in our research program. Topics not treated in our research, but which are sometimes included in the preceding descriptive formula, are those pertaining to the nature of the *medium* and the *situation* in which the communication is given. It will also be noted that all of the studies are concerned with the problems encountered when an audience is available to a communicator and do not deal with the prior problem of securing or enlarging the audience.

To indicate the general context within which the specific researches were conducted, each chapter contains a "Background" section. Following the presentation of "Research Evidence" bearing on each topic, there is an "Implications" section containing discussion of related aspects of the problem and suggestions for further research. In discussing our own results and those of prior investigators we shall attempt to indicate some of the general theoretical problems within the field. But such discussions do not by any means constitute a systematic theory of persuasion or opinion change. Rather they serve to indicate some of the issues which must be considered in constructing a general science of communication.

The major topics to be treated are presented under the following headings:

1. The Communicator. An important factor influencing the effectiveness of a communication is the person or group perceived as originating the communication—and the cues provided as to the trustworthiness, intentions, and affiliations of this source. In extreme instances, merely perceiving a particular source as advocating the new opinion will be sufficient to induce acceptance. This is generally referred to as "prestige suggestion." In most of the persuasive communications of daily life, however, the communication includes auxiliary contents, such as appeals and arguments, which operate as incentives for inducing opinion change. In such instances, the nature of the source may affect the way in which the audience responds to these auxiliary incentives. The aspects of the problem with which our investigations have been concerned are the effects of variations in the trustworthiness and expertness of the communicator on the recipients' evaluation of the presentation and on their acceptance of the position advocated by the communicator. These topics will be dealt with in Chapter 2.

2. *Content of the Communication. A. Motivating appeals.* This class of stimuli consists of communication contents which arouse emotional states or which are capable of providing strong incentives for acceptance of the new opinion and/or rejection of the original opinions held by the audience. Theoretical problems concerning the use of one major class of incentives—fear-arousing appeals—will be discussed in relation to available research findings in Chapter 3.

B. Organization of persuasive arguments. The types of arguments employed and their manner of organization will influence what the audience thinks about during exposure to a communication and hence may have a marked effect on its acceptance or rejection. The type of argument and the order of presentation may either facilitate or interfere with rehearsal of both new and old opinions. A number of selected problems concerning the organization of arguments are examined in Chapter 4: implicit as compared with explicit statement of the conclusion, presentation of one side versus two sides of an issue, and primacy versus recency effects produced by different orderings of the arguments.

3. *Audience Predispositions. A. Group conformity motives.* The influence exerted by a communicator and by what he says is often dependent upon the individual's adherence to group norms or standards. Thus, one of the important sets of audience predispositions concerns the conformity motives which stem from membership in, or affiliation with, various social groups. Predispositional factors underlying resistance to communications which advocate nonconformity will be discussed in Chapter 5, focusing particularly upon the individual's valuation of group membership. The effects of certain situational stimuli upon the strength of group conformity motives are also considered.

B. Individual personality factors. Some individuals are likely to be highly responsive to persuasion while others are more resistant. These individual differences in susceptibility to persuasion may arise from differences in abilities (e.g., capacity for comprehending the meaning of what others say) or in motives (e.g., strong desire to avoid considering adverse consequences stressed by communicator). Chapter 6 will discuss hypotheses and evidence concerning the relationship of persuasibility to general intellectual ability and to various personality factors which reflect motivational tendencies.

4. *Responses. A. Overt expression of the new opinion.* If a persuasive communication is effective, there is often a change in the individual's overt verbal behavior such that he regularly expresses the new opinion whenever a pertinent situation arises. As mentioned earlier, however, a person may sometimes be induced to conform verbally, thus overtly expressing the recommended opinion, but

without inner conviction. Nevertheless, even when only superficial conformity occurs (e.g., by inducing the individual to play a social role), the overt expression of the new opinion may have some effect on inner acceptance. In Chapter 7 a series of studies on this aspect of opinion change will be described, together with various hypotheses concerning the ways in which the effects of overt verbalization are mediated.

B. Retention of opinion change. When the recipients of a communication consistently express the new opinion, especially where there are no external constraints making for overt conformity, the inference is that the communication has produced acceptance of the new opinion. But there are a number of problems concerning the degree to which such opinions are subsequently retained. For example, powerful sources of interference may arise from subsequent exposure to competing communications which foster rejection of the opinions recommended in the first communication. Even with no subsequent counterpressure, an individual may forget the incentive material learned from the communication, so that after a short period he fails to recall those ideas favoring continued acceptance. On the other hand, the individual may initially show great resistance during the communication but subsequently appear to accept it "spontaneously." Various factors which facilitate or interfere with the persistence of opinion change are discussed in Chapter 8.

CHARACTERISTICS OF COMMUNICATION LEARNING

In the foregoing discussion, we have assumed that the effectiveness of persuasive communications is a matter of learning. To some extent, we would expect to find that there are common principles which apply equally to the learning of new opinions, of various verbal and motor skills, and of other habits. But it is necessary to recognize that the *type* of learning and the *conditions* of learning are ordinarily quite different in the case of producing opinion change through persuasive communication than in the case of other learning situations.

In his preface to Klapper's recent book [6] Lazarsfeld has emphasized the difficulties involved in taking results from laboratory studies of human learning and applying them to the presentation of persuasive communications via mass media, where the audience may "leave the field" if uninterested. He characterizes the mass communication situation as one equivalent to "a learning experiment where people walk in and out as they please, where some of the most valuable effects are achieved with people who come in by mere accident, where the motivation to learn is often very low and where the possible rewards for learning are obvious neither to the experimenter nor to the subject . . ." (Klapper, Foreword, pp. 6 and 7).

The utilizer of mass communications often has an antecedent problem with which our research has not been concerned, that of attracting an audience in the first place. But even when persuasive arguments are presented to a relatively "captive" audience—for example, to delegates at a political convention—there are still a number of unique features which make the learning situation different from academic teaching or from skill instruction in which new verbal habits are acquired:

1. When formal instruction is given, the audience ordinarily is set to learn, and voluntarily accepts the status of students in relation to an instructor. This is

generally not the case with persuasive communications in everyday life.

2. In many situations of verbal learning, as in courses on science, a major goal is to teach a large number of facts and propositions. In order to attain this objective, a great deal of practice is necessary before the individual can memorize and retain all of the information which he is expected to learn. In the case of persuasive communications, however, the recommended opinion generally consists of a single statement which is within the memory span of most individuals and in many instances a single communication is sufficient to induce opinion change. During exposure to the communication, the audience may rehearse the recommended opinion several times, but sometimes only once is sufficient for the simple task of memorizing the recommended conclusion. The main problem for the communicator, of course, is to induce the audience to accept. Thus, routine practice plays a smaller role in this type of learning. On the other hand, while one-trial learning may be within the repertoire of the learner, the communicator must often provide the special kind of practice necessary for "transfer of training," so that the learner will apply the new opinion in the many different situations in which it is subsequently relevant.

3. The retention of verbally mediated skills or of memorized verbal material sometimes suffers interference from the subsequent practice of new responses to the same stimuli. Generally speaking, however, it seldom happens that, following formal instruction, the individual is exposed to competing instruction designed to break down the new verbal habits which he has just acquired. In the case of persuasive communications dealing with

controversial opinions, on the other hand, this type of interference occurs fairly frequently. Shortly after being exposed to one communication, the audience is likely to be exposed to additional communications presenting completely different points of view and designed to create completely different opinions. Hence, the long-run effectiveness of a persuasive communication depends not only upon its success in inducing a momentary shift in opinion but also upon the sustained resistance it can create with respect to subsequent competing pressures.

From the above discussion it is apparent that there may be many special factors which are important to changing opinion but are of relatively little importance in formal verbal instruction. Search for some of these factors is one of the objectives of the present research. We shall return to this problem in the concluding chapter.

Before a comprehensive theory of communications can be constructed, it will be necessary to identify and understand the major communication variables. To this end, attention must be devoted to laying the necessary groundwork of empirical propositions concerning the relationships between communication stimuli, audience predispositions, and opinion change. The present volume represents the outcome of a continuing research project which aims at isolating key variables and providing an initial framework for subsequent theory building. To further the latter objective, we shall not only include hypotheses and experimental results but also point out some of the implications for developing in the future a general theory of communication and persuasion.

REFERENCES

1. Doob, L. W. The behavior of attitudes. *Psychol. Rev.*, 1947, 54, 135–156.
2. Festinger, L. Informal social communication. *Psychol. Rev.*, 1950, 57, 271–282.
3. Hovland, C. I. Social communication. *Proc. Am. Philos. Soc.*, 1948, 92, 371–375.
4. Hovland, C. I., Lumsdaine, A. A., and Sheffield, F. D. *Experiments on mass communication.* Princeton Univ. Press, 1949.
5. Hull, C. L. *Principles of behavior.* New York, Appleton-Century, 1943.
6. Klapper, J. T. *The effects of mass media.* New York, Columbia Univ. Bureau of Applied Social Research, 1949. (Mimeo.)
7. Lewin, K. *Field theory in social science,* D. Cartwright, ed. New York, Harper, 1951.
8. Merton, R. K., and Kitt, Alice S. Contributions to the theory of reference group behavior. In R. K. Merton and P. F. Lazarsfeld, eds. *Continuities in social research.* Glencoe, Ill., Free Press, 1950.
9. Miller, N. E., and Dollard, J. *Social learning and imitation.* New Haven, Yale Univ. Press, 1941.
10. Mowrer, O. H. *Learning theory and personality dynamics.* New York, Ronald Press, 1950.
11. Newcomb, T. M. *Social psychology.* New York, Dryden Press, 1950.
12. Sherif, M. *An outline of social psychology.* New York, Harper, 1948.
13. Smith, B. L., Lasswell, H. D., and Casey, R. D. *Propaganda, communication, and public opinion.* Princeton Univ. Press, 1946.

Rhetoric—Old and New

KENNETH BURKE

Kenneth Burke (1897-   )—writer, lecturer, literary and
music critic, translator, and teacher—was born in Pennsylvania
and educated at Ohio State and Columbia Universities; has
taught at the University of Chicago, Syracuse University, the
New School for Social Research, and Bennington College;
and is author of, among many other things, *The White Oxen
and Other Stories* (1924), *Counter-Statement* (1931), *Per-
manence and Change* (1935), *Attitudes Toward History*
(1937), *The Philosophy of Literary Form* (1941), *A Grammar
of Motives* (1945), *A Rhetoric of Motives* (1950), and *A
Rhetoric of Religion* (1961). "Rhetoric—Old and New,"
adapted from an address delivered at the annual meeting of
the Conference on College Composition and Communication
in 1950, gives rhetoric the broadest scope possible: anything
that anyone does—verbally or nonverbally, consciously or
unconsciously, for persuasion (the old rhetoric) or for identification (the new rhetoric)—is, in Burke's view, a rhetorical
"strategy." What is more, though this essay draws insights
from what Burke calls "the 'new sciences'" (anthropology
and psychology, for example), it is the most speculative essay
in this collection; in this respect, it and the essay by Hovland,
Janis, and Kelley are polar.

ON the assumption that writing and the criticism of writing have an area in common, this statement is offered in the hopes that, though presented from the standpoint of literary criticism, it may be found relevant to the teaching of communication.

Let us, as a conceit, imagine a dialogue between two characters: "Studiosus" and "Neurosis." Studiosus would be somewhat of a misnomer for the first figure, who represents a not very interested member of a freshman class taking a required course in composition; and Neurosis would be his teacher. Studiosus has complained bitterly of the work which the course requires of him, whereupon Neurosis delivers a passionate oration in defense of his subject (naturally without mention of a flitting fantasy he sometimes entertains, according to which he has been granted some *other* cross to bear).

Imagining his apology, we found it falling into three stages, that corresponded roughly to an Inferno, a Purgatorio, and a Paradiso. First would be an account of the abysmal problems that beset the use of language. Next would come a movement of transition, whereby the very sources of lamentation could, if beheld from a different angle, be transformed into the promissory. This would be the purgatorial stage. And, despite the mournfulness of our times, a glorious paradisiac ending seemed feasible, if we did a certain amount of contriving—but let us put off for a bit the description of this third stage, while we prepare for it by first giving the broad outlines of the other two.

The first stage would stress the great deceptions of speech. As with Baudelaire's sonnet on "Correspond-

From *Journal of General Education*, V (April, 1951), 203–209. Reprinted by permission of the *Journal of General Education* and the author.

ences," it would note how men wander through "forests of symbols." Man a symbol-using animal. Expatiate on the fog of words through which we stumble, perhaps adding an image (the dog and the waterfall heard enigmatically beyond the mist). Here we would consider the problems of news: the *necessary* inadequacy of the report, even in the case of the *best* reporting; the bungling nature of the medium; the great bureaucratic dinosaurs of news-collecting; the added risks that arise from the *dramatic* aspects of news. (And to get a glimpse of what sinister practices we do accept as the norm, where international relations are concerned, imagine a prize fight reported in the style regularly used for news of international disputes: one fighter's blows would be reported as threats and provocations, while the other's were mentioned in the tonalities proper to long-suffering and calm retaliation regrettably made necessary by the outlandish aggressiveness of the opponent.)

We hoped next to work in a reference to what we like to call the "scene-act" ratio. That is, a situation may be so described that one particular kind of act or attitude is implicit in it (described not falsely, but with "honest selectivity"). For a complex situation may without untruth be so reported that exclusively pugnacious rather than friendly or meditative attitudes are evoked; or the exact opposite may be as true—a rhetorical function thus lurking beneath the level of the report's "factuality." And when each day's "reality" is "dramatically" put together for us by enterprises that comb the entire world for calamities, conflicts, and dire forebodings, such a documentary replica of the arena confuses us as to the actual *recipe* of motives on which the world is operating. The most critical consideration of all is thus drastically slighted, namely, the *proportions* of the ingredients in a motivational cluster.

Given the conditions of our talk, we should pass over this stage rapidly. But before going into the second or purgatorial stage, I'd like to pause for an aside. I submit that this is the situation, as regards the present state of literary criticism: When aesthetic criticism came in, there was a corresponding demotion of rhetoric. Rhetoric was exiled. And, emigrating, it received a home among various so-called "new sciences." (Anthropology, social psychology, sociology, psychoanalysis, semantics, and the like all took over portions of it. I would also include here psychosomatic medicine, concerned as it is with ways in which our very physiques are led to take on attitudes in keeping with the rhetorical or persuasive aspects of ideas—attitudes of such conviction that they are worked into the very set of nerves, muscles, and organs.)

I shall cite one example of the way in which the "new sciences" took over: Anthropology now considers, under the heading of "magic," many symbolic devices for the establishing of social cohesion. Under the earlier dispensation, these would have been considered as aspects of *rhetoric*. But here is the paradox: After these topics were exiled and renamed "magic," literary critics who borrowed the new terms were accused by purists of importing alien perspectives into their special discipline. Accordingly, by a "new" rhetoric, we mean one designed to restore structures maimed by the vandalism of the exclusively aesthetic (an aesthetic stress, by the way, that had also made positive gains, though they are not our concern at the moment).

If I had to sum up in one word the difference between

the "old" rhetoric and a "new" (a rhetoric reinvigorated by fresh insights which the "new sciences" contributed to the subject), I would reduce it to this: The key term for the old rhetoric was "persuasion" and its stress was upon deliberate design. The key term for the "new" rhetoric would be "identification," which can include a partially "unconscious" factor in appeal. "Identification" at its simplest is also a deliberate device, as when the politician seeks to identify himself with his audience. In this respect, its equivalents are plentiful in Aristotle's *Rhetoric*. But identification can also be an end, as when people earnestly yearn to identify themselves with some group or other. Here they are not necessarily being acted upon by a conscious external agent, but may be acting upon themselves to this end. In such identification there is a partially dreamlike, idealistic motive, somewhat compensatory to real differences or divisions, which the rhetoric of identification would transcend.

But we are now ready for our second stage. For, if identification includes the realm of transcendence, it has, by the some token, brought us into the realm of transformation, or dialectic. A rhetorician, I take it, is like one voice in a dialogue. Put several such voices together, with each voicing its own special assertion, let them act upon one another in co-operative competition, and you get a dialectic that, properly developed, can lead to views transcending the limitations of each. At which point, to signalize his change of heart, poor Neurosis might now be renamed "Socraticus."

Socraticus could point out how the very lostness of men in their symbolic quandaries has led to the invention of miraculously ingenious symbolic structures—whereat the very aspects of language we might otherwise fear can become engrossing objects of study and appreciation; and works once designed to play upon an audience's passions, to "move" them rhetorically toward practical decisions beyond the work, can now be enjoyed for their ability to move us in the purely poetic sense, as when, hearing a lyric or seeing a sunrise, we might say, "How moving!" (We here touch upon the kind of heightened or elevated diction discussed in Longinus' *On the Sublime*.)

Considering the relation between rhetoric and dialectic, we come with Socraticus upon the Platonic concern with the Upward Way (linguistic devices whereby we may move from a world of disparate particulars to a principle of one-ness, an "ascent" got, as the semanticists might say, by a movement toward progressively "higher levels of generalization"). Whereat there could be a descent, a Downward Way, back into the world of particulars, all of which would now be "identified" with the genius of the unitary principle discovered en route. (All would be thus made consubstantial by participation in a common essence, as with objects bathed in the light of the one sun, that shines down upon them as from the apex of a pyramid. And the absence of such dialectic journeys on the grand scale should not be allowed to conceal from us the fact that we are continually encountering fragmentary variants of them. For instance, you may look upon a world of disparate human beings; you can next "rise to a higher level of generalization" by arriving at some such abstraction as "economic man"; and, finally, you can look upon these unique human beings simply in terms of this one attribute, thus "identifying" them with a unitary term got by a tiny rise toward generalization and a descent again from it.)

But the mention of the pyramid can lead us nicely into

the third state, our Paradiso. Socraticus might now even change his name to "Hierarchicus"—and we might dwell upon the double nature of hierarchy. Thus there is the purely verbal ascent, with corresponding resources of identification (our notion being that a rhetorical structure is most persuasive when it possesses full dialectical symmetry—or, otherwise put, dialectical symmetry is at once the perfecting and transcending of rhetoric). But there is also another line of ascent; and this involves the relation between the dialectics of identification and hierarchic structure in the social, or sociological, sense (society conceived as, roughly, a ladder, or pyramid, of interrelated roles).

Here we would consider how matters of prestige (in the old style, "wonder," or in the terminology of Corneille, "admiration") figure in the ultimate resources of "identification." Here we would note how our ideas of "beauty," and even "nature," are "fabulous," concealing within themselves a social pageantry. Here would be the ultimate step in the discussion of the ways in which man walks among "forests of symbols."

Then, for the localizing of our thesis, we might have Neurosis-Socraticus-Hierarchicus cite Castiglione's *Book of the Courtier* as a neat instance of the merger of the two dialectical series: the verbal and the social pyramids. For it deals with questions of courtly ascent, while rising through four successive stages from the mere quest of personal advancement, to a concern with the insignia of the courtier as expert or specialist, thence to the cult of courtly sexual relations, and on to the vision of an *ultimate* courtship. In this fourth stage we move into a sacrificial order of motives, fittingly introduced in the dialogues by talk of death, so that, in contrast with the earlier analysis of laughter, there is now a solemn note.

This fourth section deals, first, with the Socratic erotic, the love of truth, beauty, goodness, as seen in terms of the courtier who is now in a pedagogic role, aiming not at his own advantage but at the education of the prince in ways that will be beneficial to mankind as a whole.

After the pages on the courtier as educator of the prince, you will recall, through appropriate transitions the work rises to its exhilarating close, the oration by Cardinal Bembo, on Beauty as "an influence of the heavenly bountifulness." Here is, to perfection, the device of *spiritualization*. So, by the time the Cardinal is finished, we have gone from the *image* of beauty to the pure *idea* of beauty—we have united with ideal beauty: the courtly, truth, utility, goodness—finally we arrive at talk of the soul, which is given "to the beholding of its own substance," a substance angelic (the soul kindled by the desire to partake of the heavenly nature), where-at, with images of mounting and burning and coupling, we end on a prayer to "the father of true pleasures, of grace, peace, lowliness, and goodwill," and on talk of hopes to "smell those spiritual savors"—and lo! after the Cardinal has paused, "ravished and beside himself," we discover that the discussion has continued until dawn, so that the company, edified,

saw already in the East a fair morning like unto the color of roses, and all stars voided, saving only the sweet Governess of Heaven, Venus which keepeth the bounds of night and day, from which appeared to blow a sweet blast, that filling the air with a biting cold, began to quicken the tunable notes of the pretty birds, among the hushing woods of the hills.

Since this work is so exalted in its closing pages, like the final rejoicing of a symphonic finale, we thought we should contrive to end our apology on that. For it would be something that even Studiosus might readily applaud; and in applauding the citation, he might seem to be applauding the speaker.

But at that stage, we grew uneasy. Even suppose our ruse had succeeded. What of the morrow? What had we considered, as regards particular, practical problems?

To meet that question, we should go back to a hint introduced, in passing, when we mentioned the earlier stages of Castiglione's book. For there the author considers at great length the approved devices whereby the courtier can translate his aptitudes into schemes, stratagems, advantage-seeking actions. Can we not, when looking at the resources of words, seek to categorize and describe in that spirit the kinds of role which, while they impinge upon the rhetorical devices considered in Books vii, viii, and ix of Quintilian, have also a more personalized dimension? These would fall across all the three levels we have considered in our little Human Comedy.

Aristotle treated rhetoric as purely verbal. But there are also areas of overlap (making for a kind of "administrative" rhetoric). Consider, for instance, Machiavelli's *Prince,* as seen in this light:

Machiavelli's *The Prince* can be treated as a rhetoric insofar as it deals with the *producing of effects upon an audience.* Sometimes the prince's subjects are his audience, sometimes the rulers or inhabitants of foreign states are the audience, sometimes particular factions within the State. If you have a political public in mind, Machiavelli says in effect, here is the sort of thing you must do to move them for your purposes. And he considers such principles of persuasion as these: either treat well or crush; defend weak neighbors and weaken the strong; where you foresee trouble, provoke war; don't

make others powerful; be like the prince who appointed a
harsh governor to establish order (after this governor had
become an object of public hatred in carrying out the prince's
wishes, the prince got popular acclaim by putting him to
death for his cruelties); do necessary evils at one stroke, pay
out benefits little by little; sometimes assure the citizens that
the evil days will soon be over, at other times goad them to
fear the cruelties of the enemy; be sparing of your own and
your subjects' wealth, but be liberal with the wealth of others;
be a combination of strength and stealth (lion and fox);
appear merciful, dependable, humane, devout, upright, but
be the opposite in actuality, whenever the circumstances require it; yet always do lip-service to the virtues, since most
people judge by appearances; provoke resistance, to make an
impression by crushing it; use religion as a pretext for con-
quest, since it permits of "pious cruelty"; leave "affairs of
reproach" to the management of others, but keep those "of
grace" in your hands; be the patron of all talent, proclaim
festivals, give spectacles, show deference to local organizations; but always retain the distance of your rank (he could
have called this the "mystery" of rule); in order that you may
get the advantage of good advice without losing people's
respect, give experts permission to speak frankly, but only
when asked to speak; have a few intimates who are encour-
aged to be completely frank, and who are well plied with
rewards.[1]

As an instance of more purely literary tactics, we
might cite this passage from Demetrius' *On Style*:[2]

In fine, it is with language as with a lump of wax, out of
which one man will mould a dog, another an ox, another a
horse. One will deal with his subject in the way of exposition

[1] See the author's *Rhetoric of Motives* (New York: Prentice-Hall,
1949), p. 158.
[2] v. 296–97, Loeb ed., trans. W. Rhys Roberts (Cambridge: Harvard
University Press, 1946), p. 481.

and asseveration, saying (for example) that "men leave property to their children, but they do not therewith leave the knowledge which will rightly use the legacy." [This he calls the method of Aristippus of Cyrene.] . . . Another will (as Xenophon commonly does) express the same thought in the way of precept, as "men ought to leave not only money to their children, but also the knowledge which will use the money rightly."

What is specifically called the "Socratic" manner . . . would recast the foregoing proposition in an interrogative form, somewhat as follows. "My dear lad, how much property has your father left you? Is it considerable and not easily assessed? It is considerable, Socrates. Well now, has he also left you the knowledge which will use it rightly?"

For some years, in tentative ways, somewhat on the side, I have been trying to decide on terms for categorizing various literary strategies, as seen in the light of these borrowings from Machiavelli and Demetrius. This is no place to display the lot. But I might cite a few brief illustrations. Here, for instance, are some cullings from my notes on what I tentatively call the "bland strategy":

At one point in *The Idiot,* Ippolit accuses Mishkin of learning how to "make use of his illness." Mishkin, he says, has managed to offer friendship and money "in such an ingenious way that now it's impossible to accept under any circumstances." Mishkin's behavior has been "either too innocent or too clever." Ippolit is here in effect giving the formula for blandness. Blandness is ironic, in that the underlying meaning is the opposite of the one that shows on its face, while there is always the invitation to assume that the surface meaning is the true one.

Diplomats often use it, when sending warships abroad in times of peace. Though the warships may be dispatched purely for purposes of threat, the enterprise can be blandly put forward as a "goodwill mission." Or a government may use troop movements as a threat, and blandly call attention to the troop movements by announcing that they are but part of a "routine action" and are not intended as a threat.

A friend said: "I once had an uncle who was gentle enough, but enjoyed watching fist fights among children. Each Saturday he would get a dollar of his pay changed into pennies; and calling the children of the neighborhood, he would toss the pennies one by one, while explaining unctuously: 'Just scramble for the pennies, and each of you can keep as many as he gets. But no pushing, no shoving, boys, and above all, no fighting.' While thus setting up conditions of the Scramble that almost automatically made for a fight, he could blandly call for peace, confident that war would come before he had tossed a dozen pennies."

Or there was the case of Joseph, who, without funds, had married a rich Josephine. At first, in all simplicity, he paid for his keep by being assiduously attentive. Then slowly over the years, a perverse, and even morbid blandness emerged in his treatment of her, unbeknownst to them both. Joseph began to plague Josephine with his worries for her welfare. He did not let her live a moment without the feel of a doctor's hand on her pulse. He was so attentive that no one could fail to comment on his devotion. And in her unexpressed and inexpressible desire to poison him, she felt so guilty that each day she became more sickly. Here was a situation worthy of the André Gide who wrote *The Immoralist*. Blandness could go no further.

Soon after our occupation of Japan in the last war, Japanese officials exploited a blandness of this sort. They confounded the victors by being painfully meticulous in their desire to co-operate. They never tired of asking for "clarifications" of military orders, so that they might obey to the last letter.

They were even "scrupulous" in reporting their own violations and misunderstandings of any order. They were so assiduously anxious to please, that they made the conqueror sick of his own commands. For instead of resisting the regulations, they tirelessly brought up bothersome questions supposedly intended to "help put the regulations into effect."

An ironically bland kind of co-operation is said to have taken place during the German invasion of Czecho-Slovakia. The Nazis had been sending spies among the Czechs. These spies would spot anti-Nazi patriots by going to Czech cafes and talking "confidentially" against Hitler. Soon the Czechs learned of the ruse. Hence, next phase: Nazi spy comes to cafe where Czech patriots are gathered. In the role of *agent provocateur,* the spy talks against Hitler. Whereupon the Czechs virtuously pummel him "for saying such things against the Führer."

Given blandness enough, one person might co-operate another off the map.

Such stratagems, instances of which I have been collecting (still using a somewhat experimental terminology of placement, not logically schematized—at least not yet), sometimes apply to a rhetoric of human relations in general; sometimes they are confined to purely literary tactics. Many taken from the press fall halfway between a purely "verbal" and an "administrative" rhetoric. And many taken from books (thus from the realm of literature) at the same time have social relevance generally.

I might cite a few more places where concerns of this sort are observable.

In *The Making of Americans* Gertrude Stein came close to a systematic study of rhetorical devices in personal relations. Toward the end, for instance, when discussing how sensitiveness becomes transformed into suspicion, making a "simple thing" look like a "complicated thing," she writes:

These then I am now describing who are completely for themselves suspicious ones, who have it in them to have emotion in them become suspicious before it is a real emotion of anything for anything about anything in them, these have it completely to be certain that every one is doing feeling seeing the thing that one is feeling doing seeing believing when such a one is not agreeing with them, when such a one is feeling thinking believing doing anything that such a one is doing that thing for a mean or wicked or jealous or stupid or obstinate or cursed or religious reason, it is not a real feeling believing seeing realizing, that this one having suspicion in him is certain.

She then gives the paradigm of an anecdote:

One of such a kind of one once liked very well some one and then that one forgot to give this one five cents that this one had paid for that one and then this one hated that one, had no trust in that one for this one was certain that that one knowing that this one was too sensitive to be asking did not think it necessary to pay that one, he never could believe that any one forgot such a thing. This is an extreme thing of a way of feeling that is common to all of these of them.

The stress here moves rather toward the agent than the act (that is, in our terms, it is idealistic); but underlying it is clearly the concern with social tactics (which, one notes, her style is well adapted for stating in *generalized* form).

In a satiric epigram leveled at Cato the Censor, who had walked out of the theater in righteous indignation, Martial asks rhetorically: "Why did you come to the theater? That you might leave?"

In Aristotle's *Rhetoric* a similar pattern is considered when he notes,[3] as a "topic," that one person may make a present of something to another, in order to cause him pain by depriving him of it. Then Aristotle goes on to show how the device may be given cosmological proportions; he cites from an unknown author: "It is not from benevolence that the deity bestows great blessings upon many, but in order that they may suffer heavier calamities"—and whether or not this be a favorite device of the gods, it is certainly a device of a sort that should properly be fitted into a collection of strategies for characterizing the antics of the Human Comedy.

Proust's work is full of such concerns. The kind of closely interwoven relationships he deals with makes for tiny replicas of the stratagems used in the manipulating of mighty empires. Thus Proust notes that the servant Françoise and Aunt Eulalie are related as quarry to hunter, so that "they could never cease from trying to forestall each other's devices." And after describing the nature of their sparring, he concludes:

a middle-aged lady in a small country town, by doing no more than yield wholehearted obedience to her own irresistible eccentricities, and to a spirit of mischief engendered by the utter idleness of her existence, could see, without ever having given a thought to Louis XIV, the most trivial occupations of her daily life, her morning toilet, her luncheon, her afternoon nap, assume, by virtue of their despotic singularity, something of the interest that was to be found in what Saint Simon used to call the "machinery" of life at Versailles; and was able, too, to persuade herself that her silence, a shade of good humour or of arrogance on her features, would provide Françoise with matter for a mental commentary as tense with

[3] 2. 23.

passion and terror, as did the silence, the good humour or the arrogance of the King when a courtier, or even his greatest nobles, had presented a petition to him, at the turning of an avenue, at Versailles.

Nor was Françoise lacking in ability to wage the same kinds of warfare against underlings who were, in turn, subject to *her* jurisdiction. After referring to Fabre's descriptions of a wasp that paralyzes an insect and deposits its eggs in the victim, Proust continues:

in the same way Françoise had adopted, to minister to her permanent and unfaltering resolution to render the house uninhabitable to any other servant, a series of crafty and pitiless stratagems. Many years later we discovered that, if we had been fed on asparagus day after day, throughout that whole season, it was because the smell of the plants gave the poor kitchen-maid, who had to prepare them, such violent attacks of asthma that she was finally obliged to leave my aunt's service.

We could well cite Mark Twain as a source for a rhetoric of such devices. His concern with ruses, stratagems, with the lore of gamblers, swindlers, and the like, is not so much *moralistic* as *appreciative*. His roving enterprisers are not merely salesmen; they are rogues and spellbinders, preferably given to selling poor stuff grandiloquently.

Typically, Twain quotes this example of spiritualization, from a "now forgotten book," about a "big operator":

He appears to have been a most dexterous as well as consummate villain. When he traveled, his usual disguise was that of an itinerant preacher; and it is said that his discourses were very "soul-moving"—interesting the hearers so much that they forgot to look after their horses, which were carried away by his confederates while he was preaching.

Deflection is a particularly important device. In a sense any slight bias or even unintended error in our vocabulary for describing reality serves as a deflection. Since even the most imaginative, intelligent, virtuous, and fortunate of men must err in their attempts to characterize reality, some measure of deflection is natural, inevitable. Deflection is so perennially effective when deliberately used, because it arises so spontaneously. The Freudian notion of "displacement" in dreams indicates how close it is to the roots of natural human evasiveness.

Thus a child, provoked when made to give his brother something that he wanted to keep, began crying bitterly because his brother hadn't said "Thank you." His brother promptly said "Thank you," whereupon the child cried all the louder, "because he didn't say it soon enough."

A variant of deflection is used constantly in jokes, where two infractions are involved, one important, one trivial, and laughter is elicited by shifting the stress to the trivial one when the important one was, of course, the real issue.

A typical kind of spontaneous deflection arises thus: Wherever there is control along with disorder, the control can be blamed for the disorder. But if controls are relaxed and there is disorder, the blame can be laid to the absence of controls. Since both the controls and the relaxed controls are matters of government, it follows that government can be blamed for everything.

There is no time now for us to consider the various formulations we have tentatively used in classifying the devices. But we would like to say a few words on one of these, already mentioned in passing. And it will bring our discussion to a close. This is the device of "spiritualization," or the *nostrum* (which transcends the conflicts of the *mine* and the *thine*, the *meum* and *tuum*, by raising them to resonant terms of *ours*, the *nostrum*). Here is a grand device, central to polemic, which is forever translating back and forth between materialist and idealist terms for motives.

Are things disunited in "body"? Then unite them in "spirit." Would a nation extend its physical dominion? Let it talk of spreading its "ideals." Do you encounter contradictions? Call them "balances." Is an organization in disarray? Talk of its common *purpose*. Are there struggles over means? Celebrate agreement on ends. Sanction the troublously manifest, the incarnate, in terms of the ideally, perfectly invisible and intangible, the divine.

In a society beset by many conflicts of interests and aiming with the help of verbal tactics to transcend those conflicts, the uses of spiritualization as a device are endless. Spiritualization is the device par excellence of the Upward Way—vibrant with the gestures of unification, promise, freedom. And so, ending upon it (by recalling snatches, fragments, of Castiglione's symphonic finale):

. . . beauty . . . truth . . . utility . . . goodness . . . [all grandly united] . . . spiritual savors . . . in the East a fair morning like unto the color of roses . . . the sweet Governess of Heaven, Venus which keepeth the bounds of night and day . . . the tunable notes of the pretty birds, among the hushing woods of the hills. . . .

Toward a Modern Theory of Rhetoric: A Tagmemic Contribution[*]

RICHARD E. YOUNG
AND ALTON L. BECKER

Richard E. Young (1932-   ) and Alton L. Becker (1932-
) were born in Michigan and educated at the Universities of Michigan and Connecticut. Both of them have taught English at Connecticut, both now teach it in the College of Engineering at Michigan, and both are members of the Center for Research on Language and Language Behavior there. Becker has taught also at Ripon College, from 1958 to 1961 was a Fulbright Fellow in Burma, and is also a member of the Center for South and Southeast Asian Studies at Michigan. Much of their rhetorical research has been published in *College Composition and Communication* and the *Harvard Educational Review*. Like Ohmann's, Milic's, and Sledd's essays, "Toward a Modern Theory of Rhetoric: A Tagmemic Contribution" attempts to show how linguistic theory can provide a basis for rhetorical theory; in this instance, how the trimodal tagmemic theory of Kenneth L. Pike can provide a basis for a rhetorical theory that not only explains the facts and answers the needs of modern rhetorical practice but retains three of the five categories of classical rhetoric: invention, arrangement, and style.

[*] This article was in part supported by the Center for Research on Language and Language Behavior, University of Michigan, under Contract OE 5-14036, U. S. Office of Education.

Our discussion will be adequate if it has as much clearness as the subject-matter admits of, for precision is not to be sought for alike in all discussions. . . . We must be content . . . in speaking of such subjects and with such premises to indicate the truth roughly and in outline, and in speaking about things which are only for the most part true and with premises of the same kind to reach conclusions that are no better. In the same spirit, therefore, should each type of statement be *received;* for it is the mark of an educated man to look for precision in each class of things just so far as the nature of the subject admits; it is evidently equally foolish to accept probable reasoning from a mathematician and to demand from a rhetorician scientific proofs.

ARISTOTLE, *Nicomachean Ethics i.3.1094b 12-28.*

TRANS. W. D. ROSS

I

Y EARS ago, the heart of a liberal education was the trivium of grammar, logic, and rhetoric. Modern linguistics has come to encompass more and more of this trivium, and has in the process become transformed. Traditional grammar is no longer anathema to the linguist, and linguistic description has adopted many of the techniques of logical analysis. Furthermore, linguistics is becoming increasingly interested in the analysis and description of verbal structures beyond the sentence, traditionally a rhetorical concern. It seems fitting, therefore, to explore the relationships of linguistics and rhetoric—discovering, hopefully, just what contributions a theory of language can make to a modern theory of rhetoric.

As Aristotle states in the quotation given above, the

From *Harvard Educational Review*, XXXV (Fall, 1965), 450–468. Reprinted by permission of the *Harvard Educational Review* and the authors.

nature of the subject matter imposes some constraints on the statements we make about it. It is our intention, therefore, to define the subject matter of rhetoric as it has been understood traditionally, and then to illustrate how aspects of one modern linguistic theory—tagmemics —can form the basis for a new approach to rhetorical problems. The field is broad and there are many points of contact between linguistics and rhetoric which will be passed over here. Nor can we hope to consider all linguistic points of view, each with important contributions to make. We will limit ourselves to a description of three traditional stages in the rhetorical process—invention, arrangement, and style—and then approach the problems of each stage via tagmemic theory.

There are four rhetorical traditions which, taken together, constitute the history of rhetoric. There is sophistic rhetoric, which has as its goal the effective manipulation of language without regard to truth and logic. This tradition continues in modern propaganda and in advertising techniques. There is Platonic anti-rhetoric, which stresses not the art of writing but the quality of the writer in his adherence to truth and virtue: a good writer is a good man writing. There is the rhetoric of literary criticism, which applies the categories and techniques of rhetoric to the analysis and evaluation of poetry, drama, and narration. And finally, there is Aristotelian rhetoric, which had its origins in the law courts of early Greece and which was expanded, systematized, and given a philosophic foundation by Aristotle. After being brought to perfection by Cicero and Quintilian, it constituted a basic, and at times *the* basic, discipline in Western education for fifteen hundred years. It survives today, but with greatly diminished influence. Because this is still the most complete rhetoric ever developed and because it best defines what traditionally has been the scope of rhetoric, we shall focus our attention almost exclusively on the Aristotelian tradition.

For Aristotle, rhetoric was "the faculty of observing in any given case the available means of persuasion."[1] Its immediate end was to persuade a popular audience of what is true and just; its ultimate end was to secure the cooperation necessary for a civilized society. The classical art of rhetoric consisted of five separate arts which together embraced the entire process of developing and presenting a persuasive discourse: invention, arrangement, style, memory, and delivery. As the last two concern speaking rather than writing (which has become the principal concern of modern rhetoric), we shall consider only the first three: invention, arrangement, and style.

"Invention," wrote Cicero, "is the discovery of valid or seemingly valid arguments to render one's cause plausible."[2] Rhetoricians distinguished two kinds of arguments: extrinsic arguments, which came ready-made to the writer (e.g., eyewitness testimony, documents, confessions), and intrinsic arguments. The latter were of special interest to rhetoricians because they were subject to discovery by means of a system of topics. These topics were a kind of checklist of mental acts one could use when investigating and collecting arguments on a subject (e.g., definition by genus and differentia, comparison

---

[1] Aristotle, *Rhetoric*, i.2.1355b 26–27, trans. W. D. Ross, in *The Basic Works of Aristotle*, ed. Richard McKeon (New York: Random House, 1941), p. 1329.

[2] Quoted in Wilbur S. Howell, *Logic and Rhetoric in England, 1500-1700* (Princeton, N.J.: Princeton University Press, 1956), p. 66.

and contrast, cause and effect). Certain of these topics—the "common" topics—were appropriate to all types of speech; others—the "special" topics—were appropriate to only one of the three types of speech studied in the classical system: forensic, political, or ceremonial.

Use of the topics presupposed wide learning since they were primarily a method for putting the writer in contact with knowledge which already existed. Edward Corbett has remarked that Mortimer Adler's *Syntopicon* of Great Ideas of the Western World would have been an ideal reference work for the ancient rhetorician.[3] It was the art of invention which made rhetoric the core of humanistic education until the late Renaissance.

During the Renaissance, under the influence of Bacon and Descartes, logic increasingly came to be seen not as the art of learned discourse, as it had been since Greek times, but as an instrument of inquiry. Rhetoric gradually enlarged its boundaries to include the arts of both learned and popular discourse. The process was finally completed in the nineteenth century in the work of John Stuart Mill; commenting on the proper domains of logic and rhetoric, Mill remarked that

the sole object of Logic is the guidance of one's own thoughts: the communication of those thoughts to others falls under the consideration of Rhetoric, in the large sense in which that art was conceived by the ancients. . . .[4]

This spirit of modern science which was modifying the nature of logic and the scope of rhetoric also had its effect on the art of invention. Since the seventeenth cen-

[3] Edward P. J. Corbett, *Classical Rhetoric for the Modern Student* (New York: Oxford University Press, 1965), p. 171.

[4] Quoted in Howell, p. 350.

tury, we have increasingly regarded facts and experimental evidence as the basis for sound argument, rather than relying—as did our ancestors—on the wisdom of the past. That is, we have increasingly put our faith in extrinsic arguments. We have become much more interested in techniques for discovering what is unknown than in techniques for bringing old beliefs to bear on new problems. Thus the classical art of invention has diminished in importance while the modern art of experimental inquiry has expanded immensely. But this art of inquiry is no longer a part of modern rhetoric—each academic discipline having developed its own discovery procedures. The strength and worth of rhetoric seem, however, to be tied to the art of invention; rhetoric tends to become a superficial and marginal concern when it is separated from systematic methods of inquiry and problems of content.

The second art in classical rhetoric was that of arrangement. Rhetoricians developed persuasive patterns for organizing their materials—flexible systems of slots into which appropriate categories of subject matter were fitted. One common arrangement, the Ciceronian, had six slots: the exordium; the narrative, or exposition of the problem's history; the proposition; the demonstration; the refutation of alternative propositions; and the peroration. The functions and structures of each of these slots were systematically developed and described. Arrangement was the art of distributing within this pattern the subject matter gathered in the process of invention; arrangement also involved modifying the pattern by expanding, omitting, or reorganizing the various steps to meet the needs of the audience, speaker, and subject matter. The pattern was employed in all three types of speech: forensic, political, and ceremonial.

Since rhetoric was the art of persuasion, patterns for other modes of discourse (e.g., description, exposition) were given little attention. In the seventeenth century, however, developments in science led to an increasing interest in expository prose, a movement which parallels the shift from intrinsic to extrinsic argument. Other developments, such as the decline in the power of the aristocracy and the growing importance of evangelical religion, led to a rejection of elaborate patterning and the development of simpler, more manageable rhetorical forms, though none was described in the same detail as were the classical patterns.

Implicit in classical theory was a dualistic conception of discourse. Form was treated as independent of both the subject matter and the writer. Since the Renaissance, there has been a tendency to see form as the product of a particular mind or as discoverable within the subject matter itself. In the latter case, the form of a discourse is not separable from the content—the discourse is seen as having an organic unity. In either case, the form of a work is not predictable. If form is a personal matter, or is implicit in the subject matter, the rhetorician can make fewer generalizations about arrangement. Classical rhetoric was a rhetoric of precept; in modern times it has become, for the most part, a rhetoric of practice.

Style, the third of the rhetorical arts in classical rhetoric, was largely the technique of framing effective sentences. Its function was to give clarity, force, and beauty to ideas. Although grammar was its foundation, style was clearly a separate art, concerned with the effective use of language rather than simply with the correct use. Both, however, were concerned with language at the sentence level.

Aristotle justified the study of style on practical

grounds. Ideally, rational argument alone should be sufficient to persuade. Since experience suggests that this is
often not sufficient, the art of style must be employed if
wisdom is to be persuasive. The art of style tended, however, to become an end in itself, at times preempting the
entire field of rhetoric, possibly—as in the classical conception of arrangement—because of a dualistic view in
which content and style were separable.

In the classical tradition, good style was a deliberate
departure from the speech of everyday life. Renaissance
classicists ingeniously isolated and systematized figures
of speech. Henry Peacham's *Garden of Eloquence*
(1577), for example, lists 184 schemes and tropes—
artistic departures from ordinary syntax and word meanings. Clarity and appropriateness became less frequent
constraints than elegance and ingenuity. As a result,
"rhetoric" gained its pejorative connotation of elegant
but empty verbosity.

As with the other rhetorical arts, there was a reaction
against this concept of style; rhetoricians now sought a
norm closer to the speech of everyday life. In the eighteenth century, the dualistic conception of style and
content began to compete with monistic conceptions.
Style came to mean either the characteristic expression
of a particular personality (*Le style c'est l'homme
même*) or the mode of expression organically a part of
the subject matter itself.

Since the eighteenth century, the analysis of style has
become almost exclusively the concern of literary criticism. In rhetoric courses today, style is still seen by and
large as the art of framing effective sentences; but the
art is much simpler, less systematic, and considerably
more intuitive than it was in classical rhetoric.

The classical art of rhetoric has a number of weaknesses which make it inadequate for our time. Without involving ourselves directly in a criticism of the philosophical assumptions upon which classical rhetoric is based, we can note, in general, four major problems. First, the classical art of invention stresses authoritative confirmation of present beliefs, while modern modes of inquiry stress imaginative discovery of new facts and relationships. Second, the art of arrangement includes only patterns of persuasion, and neglects considerations of form in other important rhetorical modes such as description, narration, and exposition. Third, both the art of arrangement and the art of style divorce form from content, failing to consider the importance of the act of discovery in the shaping of form. And finally, the art of style is concerned primarily with embellishing, clarifying, and giving point to sentences, an approach which neglects both the deeper personal roots of style and the ways in which style is manifested in patterns beyond the sentences.

In recent years, numerous rhetoricians have been seeking a new rhetoric which would be as effective on a practical level and as stimulating and coherent on a theoretical level as is classical rhetoric. As Daniel Fogarty puts it, there are numerous "roots for a new rhetoric."[5] While other members of the trivium have changed greatly from their earlier forms (witness the revolution in Mill's *System of Logic*, the later changes in symbolic logic, and the recent revolution in grammatical theory), there has as yet been no comparable change in rhetoric. That is, there has been no change which in-

[5] Daniel Fogarty, *Roots for a New Rhetoric* (New York: Bureau of Publications, Teachers College, Columbia University, 1959).

cludes both a complete theory and an explicit practical
method. Rhetoric is still in the midst of a chaotic transition period. I. A. Richards is right, unfortunately, when
he describes the general state of rhetoric today as

the dreariest and least profitable part of the waste that the
unfortunate travel through in Freshman English! So low has
Rhetoric sunk that we would do better just to dismiss it to
Limbo than to trouble ourselves with it—unless we can find
reason for believing that it can become a study that will
minister successfully to important needs.[6]

II

The tagmemic approach to language analysis and
description, developed primarily by Kenneth L. Pike
and his associates in the Summer Institute of Linguistics,[7] has for many years been concerned with problems
which have traditionally been within the scope of rhetoric. This concern results, in part, from the strong motivation which such a model gives for moving beyond the
specification of well-made sentences. In tagmemic theory, any linguistic unit is assumed to be well defined only
when three aspects of the unit are specified: its contrastive features, its range of variation, and its distribu-

[6] I. A. Richards, *The Philosophy of Rhetoric* (New York: Oxford
University Press, 1936), p. 3. Kenneth Burke and S. I. Hayakawa
have both developed extremely interesting theories of rhetoric and must
be mentioned, along with Richards, as having made notable contributions to the development of a new rhetoric.

[7] The basic source of tagmemic theory is Kenneth L. Pike, *Language
(in Relation to a Unified Theory of the Structure of Human Behavior)*
(Glendale, Calif.: Summer Institute of Linguistics, Part I, 1951; Part II,
1955; Part III, 1960). A new edition, to be published by Mouton, is in
preparation. Pike applies tagmemic theory to problems of rhetoric in
"Beyond the Sentence," *College Composition and Communication*, XV,
No. 3 (October, 1964), and "Discourse Analysis and Tagmeme
Matrices," *Oceanic Linguistics* (April, 1965).

tion in sequence and ordered classes. This constraint on grammatical description (defined as a description necessary and sufficient to include all relevant aspects of any linguistic unit) has meant that a complete description of sentences, for example, should include a specification of their distribution in paragraphs and other larger units of discourse.

This concern with problems which traditionally have been a part of rhetoric also results from the desire of many who use the tagmemic model to provide a means for producing extended discourse, primarily biblical translation. Translators frequently encounter instances of grammatical constraints extending beyond the sentence. In some Philippine languages, for example, there is a system of focus somewhat like active and passive voice in English though vastly more complex. To produce understandable discourse in these languages apparently requires a marked correlation between situational roles (actor, goal, instrument, setting, etc.) and grammatical roles (subject, predicate, object, locative, etc.) in a sequence of sentences.[8]

As the linguist moves beyond the sentence, he finds himself asking questions which have long concerned rhetoricians. The description of the structure of a sentence and the description of the structure of an expository paragraph, extended argument, or novel are not sharply different kinds of activity, for all involve selecting and ordering language in a significant way. The traditional separation of grammar, logic, rhetoric, and poetics begins to break down.

Selecting and ordering language, however, has two

---

[8] Kenneth L. Pike, "A Syntactic Paradigm," *Language, XXXIX* (April-June, 1963), 216–30. See also "Discourse Analysis and Tagmeme Matrices," footnote 7.

aspects. One sort of inquiry into the selection and ordering of language leads us deeply into the mental activity
of the writer and into questions which are difficult,
perhaps impossible, to answer except intuitively. Can
we specify in detail why a writer chooses to write "John
loves Mary" rather than "John is in love with Mary"?
Probably not; we can only describe the choices he does
make, the characteristic features of his style. Another
sort of inquiry, however, leads us to the conventions
which constrain the writer. We can specify the reasons
why "Love John is Mary in" does not make sense to us
except in rather far-fetched ways. In the same way, we
believe we can specify why the following sequence of
sentences does not make sense:

> The trees are budding. Coal is a form of carbon. He has
> been singing for three hours now. The world used to be round.
> It seems enough.

If we were to prod the reader, insisting that the above
"sentence" and "paragraph" do have meaning, he could
probably find some sense in them, as many have in
Chomsky's "Colorless green ideas sleep furiously." In
each case one "discovers" meaning by imposing conventional formal patterns on the deviant sequences.

Both the process of imposing pattern on (or discovering pattern in) apparently meaningless utterances and
the process of describing the conventions of language
are important to the linguist. In the former process, he
uses some sort of discovery procedure; in the latter, he
employs a descriptive model which specifies the structures of conventional utterances. Although the act of
discovery is in part intuitive, the model does provide
both a method for finding significant linguistic patterns

and a taxonomy of the sort of patterns the analyst is likely to find—the still tentative universals of language. Discovery procedures are not mechanical; there is as yet no completely systematic way of analyzing a language, just as there is no algorithm for planning an effective literary composition. But there are important guides to the processes: one can learn to analyze a language and he can learn a great deal about how to write an essay or a novel.

We believe that the procedures the linguist uses in analyzing and describing a language are in some important ways like the procedures a writer uses in planning and writing a composition, and hence that tagmemic theory can provide the basis for a new approach to rhetoric. Tagmemic discovery procedures can provide a heuristic comparable to the Aristotelian system of invention; the tagmemic descriptive model can give us a vehicle for describing conventional rhetorical patterns. If our beliefs are sound, this approach will provide a bridge between the traditionally separate disciplines of grammar and rhetoric.

A heuristic is a method of solving problems, a series of steps or questions which are likely to lead an intelligent analyst to a reasonable solution of a problem. There are two different (though related) kinds of heuristic: a taxonomy of the sorts of solutions that have been found in the past; and an epistemological heuristic, a method of inquiry based on assumptions about how we come to know something. Bacon's statement of the distinction is worth quoting:

The invention of speech or argument is not properly an invention: for to invent is to discover that we know not, and not to recover or resummon that which we already know;

and the use of this invention is no other but *out of the knowl-edge whereof our mind is already possessed, to draw forth or call before us that which may be pertinent to the purpose which we take into our consideration.* So as, to speak truly, it is no *Invention,* but a *Remembrance* or *Suggestion,* with an application; which is the cause why the schools do place it after judgment, as subsequent and not precedent. Never-theless, because we do account it a Chase as well of deer in an inclosed park as in a forest at large, and that it hath already obtained the name, let it be called invention: so as it be perceived and discerned, that the scope and end of this invention is readiness and present use of our knowledge, and not addition or amplification thereof.[9]

Aristotelian rhetoric provides a taxonomy of effective rhetorical arguments which a speaker can use to attain specific ends with specific audiences. Tagmemic theory, on the other hand, provides an epistemological heuristic.

Tagmemic epistemology is based largely on two prin-ciples, though other principles are necessary for a com-plete statement of the theory. These two principles emphasize the active role of the observer in discovering pattern, and hence meaning, in the world around him. The first principle contrasts external and internal views of human behavior—in tagmemic jargon, *etic* and *emic* views. This distinction can be seen in the differences between phonetic and phonemic contrasts in linguistic phonology. A phonetic inventory provides a systematic statement of the overt phonological distinctions which occur in various human languages, while a phonemic description provides a systematic statement of the *sig-nificant* phonological distinctions in a particular lan-guage. A distinction is judged significant, and hence phonemic, if it signals a difference in the lexical meaning

9 Quoted in Howell, p. 367.

of linguistic units. Though there is much controversy about how phonological signals are to be described, the basic distinction remains valid: the contrast, for example, between aspirated and unaspirated consonants is lexically significant for a native speaker of Hindi or Burmese but not for a native speaker of English, who has difficulty in learning to hear this contrast.

The distinction is especially important when two emic systems come in contact, as when the speaker of English is learning to speak Hindi and is forced to recognize that his native distinctions are emic and not necessarily universal. Likewise, one who finds himself in a different culture must learn to distinguish universals of human behavior from particular customs and mores which taken together comprise the emic distinctions of a culture. The ways of treating time and space, for example, vary throughout the world, and one must learn these ways if he wishes to communicate and cooperate outside his own culture.

Though it is interesting to envision a universal etics of rhetoric—an orderly classification of the rhetorical forms found throughout the world—our present concern must be with the writer of English who is writing for readers of English. Even with this restriction one confronts frequent clashes of emic systems, for if a writer has anything new to say, his image of the world must be in some way different from that of his reader. It is at this point of difference that his message lies. He may seek to expand or clarify some feature of the reader's image, thus making it more nearly like his own, or he may seek to replace some feature of the reader's image. In the first instance he would be informing; in the second, persuading.

Before developing this discussion of rhetorical intention further, we must introduce the second major principle in tagmemic epistemology. This principle asserts that a complete analysis of a problem necessitates a trimodal perspective. After the trimodal principle had been worked out in tagmemic theory and the so-called *feature, manifestation,* and *distribution* modes had been defined, Pike noted a striking similarity between these modes and the triple perspectives of modern physics— the complementary views of physical phenomena as involving particles, waves, and fields; as a consequence, Pike decided to adopt this second set of terms for his behavioral model.[10]

Language phenomena—and presumably all human behavior—can be viewed in terms of particles (discrete contrastive bits), waves (unsegmentable physical continua), or fields (orderly systems of relationships). For example, a sentence can be viewed as a sequence of separate words or morphemes; as a physical continuum consisting of acoustic waveforms; or as a system of interrelationships manifesting the grammatical, lexical, and phonological rules of English. Tagmemic theory asserts that only by this complementarity of perspectives is a complete analysis of language structure possible.

The principle of trimodalism gives the analyst both a procedure for approaching new problems and a safeguard against a too limited view of the data. Only when he has described his data from all three perspectives can he be reasonably sure that his analysis is complete. The writer, likewise, can use the principle as an aid in discov-

[10] Kenneth L. Pike, "Language as Particle, Wave, and Field," *The Texas Quarterly,* II (Summer, 1959), pp. 37–54.

ering a wide range of features in his topic. Though a writer often emphasizes one mode in a particular work, he should be aware of the other possibilities, particularly if his readers customarily emphasize a different mode. Let us consider a simple example. A particle description of a flower emphasizes those features which make it distinctive from other flowers. A wave description emphasizes the flower as a moment in a process from seed to final decay (even this is only a peak in a larger wave) or as merging into a scene. A field description may partition a flower into its functional parts or classify it in a taxonomical system. The flower may also be seen metaphorically or symbolically, in which case it is conceived as part of a new conceptual field (religious, say, or geometric), where certain of its features (its beauty or its shape) are hypostatized, allowing it to manifest a category in a new field. One can view any topic trimodally and soon discover a wide range of significant perspectives.[11] The process is broad, flexible, and intuitive, though the intuition is guided by what has proved to be a very fruitful principle. It is especially useful since it is not limited to a particular subject matter. In this sense, it is similar to the "common" topics of classical rhetoric. A generally applicable approach helps to free us from the built-in limitations of a conventional, specialized approach. Thus the discovery procedure has a corrective function also.

This heuristic procedure—based on the emic-etic distinction and trimodal perspective—both helps the writer

[11] For further illustrations of the use of tagmemic discovery procedures in rhetorical invention, see Hubert English, "Linguistics as an Aid to Invention," *College Composition and Communication*, XV, No. 3 (October, 1964).

explore his topic and generates a set of questions which he can use to analyze his reader's preconceptions, that is, his reader's emic system:

1) What are the distinctive features of the reader's conception of the topic? What characteristics does it have that lead him to contrast it with similar things? (Particle view)

2) How are the reader's views on this topic part of a mental process, a phase in the continual development of his system of values and assumptions? (Wave view)

3) How does the reader partition the topic? What are its functional elements for him? How does he classify it? (Field view)

The answers to these questions provide criteria for selecting and ordering the writer's subject matter as he develops his discourse.

The missionary linguist in the field seeks to translate his message into the language and cultural conventions of the people, not to teach them English and his own emic conventions. He does not seek to replace their emic system with his own, but to modify their image after finding within it their motivations for receiving his message.[12] For he realizes that change is most effective and enduring when it occurs within the emic system of those he is trying to convince. Unlike traditional rhetoric which sought to persuade people by confirming authoritative attitudes, modern rhetoric, we believe, must seek identification. That is, the writer must seek to have his readers identify his message with their emic system.

---

[12] Our conception of the image here is drawn in large part from Kenneth Boulding, *The Image* (Ann Arbor: University of Michigan Press, 1956), and from William Angus Sinclair, *Conditions of Knowing* (London: Routledge and Kegan Paul, 1951).

Because it seeks identification rather than persuasion, and because this assumption often leads the writer to modify his own position, modern rhetoric—still in the process of development—is characterized by Kenneth Burke and others as "discussion rhetoric." The basis for a rhetoric of this sort has been developed by Anatol Rapaport in his book *Fights, Games, and Debates,* where it is called Rogerian debate—its assumptions having been derived from the methods of the psychotherapist Carl Rogers.[13] This principle of identification of the writer with his audience points toward a rhetoric not of opposition but of mutual respect.

A comparison of emic systems—different systems of selecting and grouping followed by writer and reader—leads the writer to find what he shares with his reader in his conception of the topic and what he does not share. One of the assumptions of tagmemics is that change can occur only over the bridge of a shared element. There can be no action at a distance. The key to understanding language change, for example, is the identification of the shared features of the initial state and the subsequent altered state. The writer's message is an unshared item in the comparison, while the shared items, insofar as they are relevant to the message, provide the means by which the reader can identify—and identify with—the message. Shared items are the potential bridges over which change can take place. These bridges may be broad cultural conventions or more specific things such as common social roles, problems, or philosophical assumptions. Among the most important of these shared items is a common language—a common

[13] Anatol Rapaport, *Fights, Games, and Debates* (Ann Arbor: University of Michigan Press, 1961).

set of patterns and rules governing selection and grouping of words or morphemes within a sentence, and of
sentences and paragraphs within still larger units of
discourse. It is here that the linguist can make his unique
contribution to a new theory of rhetoric, especially as he
broadens his focus to include units larger than the
sentence.

So far we have dealt chiefly with what might be called
prewriting problems, problems of discovery. We believe,
as did Aristotle and Cicero, that a complete theory of
rhetoric must include the entire sequence of acts which
result in the finished discourse, beginning with the
initial act of mental exploration. We have offered two
principles of tagmemic heuristic as an indication, hardly
an exhaustive one, of how linguistics can contribute to
this aspect of rhetorical theory. We now turn to a description of rhetorical patterns beyond the sentence,
extending techniques which have been used in the past
in the description of lower-level patterns.

Early tagmemics was essentially, but not entirely, a
slot-and-substitution grammar, describing linguistic patterns as sequences of functional slots which are filled, or
manifested, by a class of fillers. These slots are seen as
functional parts of a pattern and may be stated in a
formula such as the following simplified formula for an
English transitive sentence:

$$+ \text{Subject} + \text{Verb} + \text{Object} \pm \text{Manner} \pm \text{Locative} \\ \pm \text{Temporal}$$

(He walked the dog slowly around the block yesterday.)
Some of these slots are obligatory ($+$), some optional
($\pm$). Each may be manifested by one of a set of filler
constructions; thus the subject slot can be filled by a

noun phrase, a pronoun, an adjective phrase, a verbal phrase, a clause, etc. More fully represented, the subject slot in the formula above would be:

+ Subject: np,p,ap,vp, ... c

Tagmemics assumes that language is composed of interlocking lexical, phonological, and grammatical hierarchies. Here, the internal surface structure of the fillers of the subject slot of the sentence are described at the clause, phrase, word, and morpheme levels of the grammatical hierarchy.

In at least two important ways, however, recent tagmemic grammar goes beyond the surface-level descriptions of other slot-and-substitution grammars.[14] First, tagmemic grammars go on to represent the filler class of a functional slot as a multidimensionally ordered set, or, in tagmemic jargon, a matrix. The categories of these ordered sets indicate relationships of concord between one tagmeme and another; thus, the filler class of the subject tagmeme is ordered into categories such as singular-plural and human-nonhuman in concord with these same categories in the predicate, so that, for example, a singular, nonhuman subject specifies the selection of a singular, nonhuman verb, preventing such collocations as "the tree jump fences."

Second, and more important for our present discussion, tagmemic grammars specify in addition to the surface structure of patterns an ordered set of operations to be carried out on the patterns. These include ordered

[14] A full description of tagmemic grammatical theory can be found in Robert Longacre, *Grammar Discovery Procedures* (The Hague: Mouton, 1964). Tagmemics is contrasted with transformational and other models in Longacre, "Some Fundamental Insights of Tagmemics," *Language*, XLI, No. 1 (January-March, 1965), pp. 65–76.

reading rules by which all possible readings of a formula are generated. Then each reading is reordered according to permutation rules. Finally, in each reading and its permuted variants, the tagmeme symbols are replaced by each of the possible filler constructions according to a set of exponence rules. These operations are carried out repeatedly until only morphemes or symbols for morpheme classes manifest the formulas, which are then terminal grammatical strings, not yet sentences until phonological and lexical specifications have been met.

Though a description of English will not specify sentences such as the one mentioned earlier, "Love John is Mary in," it so far contains no constraints to prevent it from accepting a sequence of sentences of this type:

> The trees are budding. Coal is a form of carbon. He has been singing for three hours now. The world used to be round. It seems enough.

This is not a paragraph because there is no formal connection between the sentences. We can discern no conventional pattern relating them, as we can, for example, in this pair of sentences:

> What is John doing?
> He's washing his face.

This second sequence manifests a conventional rhetorical pattern—Question-Answer. The question is marked by three formal features: the word order, the question word *what*, and (in writing) the punctuation. The second sentence is recognized as an answer to the question by: the pronoun reference (*he* has to be a.substitute for *John* here); the parallel grammatical structure, in which the functional slots of the question words in the first sentence (What . . . doing) are filled in the second (washing his face); the parallelism of verb form (is —ing); the fact that *washing* is a possible lexical equivalent for *doing*; and (in writing) the period. Question-Answer is a formal pattern illustrating a number of formal constraints which extend beyond the sentence.

The relationship of these two sentences can be described in numerous ways (probably most simply by seeing the first as a permutation of the second), but the sentences can only be described as a *sequence* by positing the larger Question-Answer pattern, and by specifying the formal ways in which the two functional slots in this larger pattern are related, just as we specify the relationship between subject and predicate in a sentence. A number of these relatively simple two-part patterns can be described, including greetings, cause and result (hypothesis), topic and illustration, topic and partition, disjunction, and so forth. These patterns can be manifested by a single sentence or by two or more sentences. A large number of higher-level units of discourse can be described as chains of these simple two-part patterns.

As we move on to larger rhetorical patterns, the complexity increases. Formal signals become redundant: for example, we can identify the Answer in the Question-Answer pattern above by five of its contrastive features. Further, lexical and semantic features become increasingly important in recognizing patterns: in the example above we recognize *washing* as a lexical equivalent of *doing*. Lexical equivalence chains are probably the most important markers of higher-level patterns.[15] We can

[15] The concept of lexical equivalence chains is derived in large part from Zellig S. Harris, *Discourse Analysis Reprints* (The Hague: Mouton, 1963), pp. 7–10.

illustrate some of this complexity by attempting to describe the paragraph as a formal structure, limiting ourselves here to only one rather simple pattern.

We believe that written paragraphs are emically definable units—not just groups of sentences isolated by rather arbitrary indentations—and that this fact can be demonstrated. We are presently carrying out controlled testing of the recognition of these units in collaboration with psychologists at the Center for Research on Language and Language Behavior, University of Michigan. Informal investigation has shown that readers, given a text in which all paragraph indentations have been removed, can successfully mark paragraph breaks, with only limited indeterminancy at predictable points. In addition, the readers are able to recognize a number of recurring paragraph patterns and to partition these patterns in predictable ways.

One of the most common of these patterns is the one we have labelled TRI (topic-restriction-illustration) or more formally,

$$+ T^2 \pm R + I^n.$$

(The raised numbers indicate that in reading the formula, T may be read twice; R, once; and I, n number of times recursively.) This is the Topic-Illustration pattern with an optional intermediary slot in which the topic is restricted in some way (e.g., by definition, classification, or partition). The following paragraph illustrates this pattern:

(T) The English Constitution—that indescribable entity—is a living thing, growing with the growth of men, and assuming ever-varying forms in accordance with the subtle and complex laws of human character. (R) It is the child of wisdom and chance. (I) The wise men of 1688 moulded it into the shape we know, but the chance that George I could not speak English gave it one of its essential peculiarities—the system of a Cabinet independent of the Crown and subordinate to the Prime Minister. The wisdom of Lord Grey saved it from petrification and set it upon the path of democracy. Then chance intervened once more. A female sovereign happened to marry an able and pertinacious man, and it seemed likely that an element which had been quiescent within it for years—the element of irresponsible administrative power— was about to become its predominant characteristic and change completely the direction of its growth. But what chance gave, chance took away. The Consort perished in his prime, and the English Constitution, dropping the dead limb with hardly a tremor, continued its mysterious life as if he had never been.[16]

The slots in this tripartite pattern are marked by lexical equivalence classes, two of which have extended domains: 1) English Constitution, indescribable entity, living thing, It, child, . . . English Constitution; 2) men, human character, wise men of 1688, George I, Lord Grey, . . . Consort. Note that the domain of the first chain is the entire paragraph, while that of the second chain is the I slot. Chains can thereby be ranked as head and attribute chains, each paragraph including a head chain and one or more attribute chains.

The slots are also marked by: grammatical parallelism (first and second sentences, third and fourth sentences); tense shift (shift to past in the I slot); pronoun domains; determiners; and transitional function words (then, but).

The TRI pattern has a number of variant forms which can be specified by the reading, permutation, and ex-

---

[16] Lytton Strachey, *Queen Victoria* (New York: Harcourt, Brace, 1921), pp. 300–301.

ponence rules. Only a few of these variants will be illustrated. Since R is optional, the pattern can be read as: $+ T + I$. For example, a paragraph by Marchette Chute:

(T) The only safe way to study contemporary testimony is to bear constantly in mind this possibility of prejudice and to put almost as much attention on the writer himself as on what he has written. (I) For instance, Sir Anthony Weldon's description of the Court of King James is lively enough and often used as source material; but a note from the publisher admits that the pamphlet was issued as a warning to anyone who wished to "side with this bloody house" of Stuart. The publisher, at any rate, did not consider Weldon an impartial witness. At about the same time Arthur Wilson published his history of Great Britain, which contained an irresistibly vivid account of the agonized death of the Countess of Somerset. Wilson sounds reasonably impartial; but his patron was the Earl of Essex, who had good reason to hate that particular countess, and there is evidence that he invented the whole scene to gratify his patron.[17]

If I is read a number of times, the pattern may be broken by indentation into more than one paragraph, although it remains a single emic unit. Indentation, like line ends in poetry, can either correspond to formal junctures or, for various reasons, can interrupt the structure in a way somewhat similar to poetic enjambment.

The TRI pattern can be permuted to IRT, producing the so-called funnel effect or inductive structure. This is comparable to such permutations at the sentence level as "Home is the sailor" from "The sailor is home." Another illustration by Marchette Chute:

[17] Marchette Chute, "Getting at the Truth," *The Saturday Review*, Sept. 19, 1953, p. 12.

(I) The reason Alice had so much trouble with her flamingo is that the average flamingo does not wish to be used as a croquet mallet. It has other purposes in view. The same thing is true of a fact, which can be just as self-willed as a flamingo and has its own kind of stubborn integrity. (R) To try to force a series of facts into a previously desired arrangement is a form of misuse to which no self-respecting fact will willingly submit itself. (T) The best and only way to treat it is to leave it alone and be willing to follow where it leads, rather than to press your own wishes upon it.[18]

This permutation is frequently used to begin or end discourse, probably because it imparts a greater sense of closure than the more open-ended TRI order.

Other permutations include TIRI, ITR, and TRIT, to list only the most common. Following exponence rules, slots in paragraph patterns may be filled by other rhetorical patterns. In the following example by Bernard Iddings Bell, the Answer slot in the Question-Answer pattern which we discussed earlier is filled by a TRI pattern, producing a compound paragraph structure:

(Q) Is the United States a nation composed chiefly of people who have not grown up, who think and act with the impulsiveness of adolescents? (A-T) Many shrewd observers of the American scene, both abroad and here at home, are saying that this is indeed the case. (R) They intentionally disturb our patriotic complacency. (I) They bid us view with alarm cultural immaturity revealed by current trends in journalism, by the radio, by the motion picture, by magazines and best-selling books, by mass response to emotionalized propaganda—political and otherwise; by a patent decay of good manners, by the spread of divorce and by other manifestations of parental irresponsibility; by all the various aspects of

[18] *Ibid.*, p. 44.

behavior which indicate to a student of human affairs the health or sickness of a civilization.[19]

Tagmemic matrix theory provides further insight into another traditional problem of rhetoric. We said earlier that form and idea are seen by many as organically unified, a view that we share. The literary statement contains within itself its own dimensions of development. It constitutes a semantic field which is clearly perceived when we try to extend it. The relevant categories of the English Constitution paragraph discussed above can be displayed in the rows and columns of an emic paragraph matrix (see Table 1).

If we were to extend the paragraph, we would be obliged to supply a still more recent illustration of the effect of wisdom on the Constitution. It should be possible from a study of a large number of paragraph matrices to generalize further about various types of paragraph development. The investigation of paragraphs as semantic fields is as yet only beginning.

A writer's style, we believe, is the characteristic route he takes through all the choices presented in both the writing and prewriting stages. It is the manifestation of his conception of the topic, modified by his audience, situation, and intention—what we might call his "universe of discourse." These variables directly affect selecting and grouping in all three linguistic hierarchies: grammatical, phonological, and lexical. An analysis and description of style involves the specification of the writer's characteristic choices at all points in the writing process, although usually only the final choices are directly accessible to the analyst.

[19] Bernard Iddings Bell, "We Are Indicted for 'Immaturity'," *New York Times Magazine,* July 20, 1947, p. 8.

The classical conception of style has a number of limitations. To see style as an addition to the message, an affective layer imposed on conventional language, ignores the close connection between language and idea.

Table 1

Forces shaping the English Constitution / historical manifestations	wisdom	chance
(1688)	The wise men . . . molded it into the shape we know	
(1714)		George I . . . gave it . . . the system of a Cabinet independent of the Crown and subordinate to the Prime Minister.
(1832)	Lord Grey saved it from petrification and set it upon the path of democracy.	
(1840)		[Victoria's marriage made it seem likely that a quiescent element] was about to become its predominant characteristic and change . . . the direction of its growth.
(1861)		[With the death of the Consort] the English Constitution . . . continued its mysterious life as if he had never been.
( )	⋮	⋮

Seeing it as essentially a matter of sentences ignores stylistic patterns beyond the sentence. In addition, the theory grew out of a very specialized sort of practice—formal public speaking in the courts and legislatures and at ceremonial gatherings. As a result it has a limited range of applicability. Seventeenth century critics were right in saying that its generalizations were inappropriate to a wide range of important topics, audiences, and situations. Finally, the highly normative approach of classical rhetoric tends to ignore the individuality of the writer, describing *a style* rather than *style* itself.

To consider style, however, (as do some modern rhetoricians) to be the expression of a particular personality lays too much stress on one variable in the universe of discourse and too little on the others. Some stylistic features of a work inevitably remain unexplained if one commits himself to this definition strictly. To see style as a vision of the topic also has limitations; it ignores the influence of situation and audience on choice. It assumes that the act of writing is essentially expressive, not communicative. Both of these views inhibit systematic theorizing about style; when style is seen as something highly personal, generalization becomes difficult.

To see style in the way many linguists do today—as deviation from conventional language—leads to the difficulty of defining conventional language. Somehow, the deviations must be separated from the corpus, perhaps by measuring the frequencies of patterns. However it is done, it leaves conventional language as a styleless language. This view, like the classical view, tends to conceive of style as an embellishment, an added affective layer. Though very unconventional styles can be identified as linguistic deviations, there are "conventional" styles which this approach does not explain. These include the different styles we all use in various situations, with various audiences, and in writing with various intents on various topics.

It seems to us that a full discussion of style must include the prewriting process if it is to interpret the formal manifestations on the written page—the purely linguistic choices that the writer has made. Without the context of a linguistic unit—the universe of discourse—we are able to describe stylistic features only in a fairly trivial way. With the context provided, there is the possibility of explaining the writer's choices. In a complete theory, then, a particular style is a characteristic series of choices throughout the entire process of writing, including both discovery (invention) and linguistic selection and grouping (arrangement).

We have presented what we believe to be the traditional problems of rhetoric and have suggested how a linguistic model which includes both a discovery procedure and a descriptive technique may provide the base for a new approach to rhetoric, a bridge between the humanities and the sciences. A tagmemic rhetoric stands somewhere between the rigorous theories of science and the almost purely intuitive theories of the humanities. We see no reason to reject the insights of either the former or the latter, believing that all new knowledge— like the process of writing itself—involves both intuitive analogy and formal precision.

A Generative Rhetoric of the Paragraph

FRANCIS CHRISTENSEN

Francis Christensen (1902-   ) was born in Utah and educated at the University of Utah and California (Berkeley) and Harvard University. He has taught at the University of Wisconsin, De Pauw University, and the University of Southern California, where he is now professor of English. He is well known for his work in the romantic movement and in stylistics. Among his other essays on rhetoric is "A Generative Rhetoric of the Sentence," *College Composition and Communication*, XIV (1963). Like Young and Becker's essay, Christensen's "A Generative Rhetoric of the Paragraph" is concerned with both the analysis and the generation or creation of paragraphs, "verbal structures beyond the sentence," and with three of the five categories of classical rhetoric: invention, arrangement, and style. *Effective* paragraphs of discursive prose have, Christensen believes, semantic unity, or unity of content (typically achieved by use of a topic sentence with other sentences semantically subordinate to it and semantically coordinate with one another); and he suggests that this semantic unity is mirrored in, or signalled by, the form of the paragraph (coordinate sentences have similar structures—"like things in like ways is one of the imperatives of discursive writing"—and sentences subordinate to them have different structures).

IN my article "A Generative Rhetoric of the Sentence" (*CCC*, October 1963), I said that the principles used there in analyzing the sentence were no less applicable to the paragraph. My purpose here is to make good that claim, to show that the paragraph has, or may have, a structure as definable and traceable as that of the sentence and that it can be analyzed in the same way. In fact, since writing that paper, I have come to see that the parallel between sentence and paragraph is much closer than I suspected, so close, indeed, that as Josephine Miles put it (in a letter) the paragraph seems to be only a macro-sentence or meta-sentence.

The chapters on the paragraph in our textbooks are so nearly alike in conception that one could almost say that, apart from the examples, the only striking difference is in the choice of *indention* or *indentation*. The prescription is always the same: the writer should work out a topic sentence and then choose one of the so-called methods of paragraph development to substantiate it. The topic sentence may appear at the beginning or at the end of the paragraph or anywhere in between, or it may be merely "implied," a sort of ectoplasmic ghost hovering over the paragraph. Besides this, some books speak of "paragraph movement"—chronological (as in narrative), spatial (as in description), logical (as in discursive writing). If the movement is logical, it may be inductive or deductive or a combination of the two, and some books offer diagrams, as systems analysts use flow charts, to picture the thought funneling down from the topic sentence or down to it.

This prescription for writers and the analysis it is

From *College Composition and Communication*, XVI (October, 1965), 144–156. With revisions, May, 1966. Reprinted with the permission of the National Council of Teachers of English and the author.

based on are even more unworkable than the conventional treatment of the sentence as simple-compound-complex, with emphasis on the complex, or as loose-balanced-periodic, with emphasis on the periodic. I doubt that many of us write many paragraphs the way we require our charges to write them or that we could find many paragraphs that exemplify the methods of development or the patterns of movement.*

First, the methods of paragraph development. These methods are real, but they are simply methods of development—period. They are no more relevant to the paragraph than, on the short side, to the sentence or, on the long side, to a run of several paragraphs or to a paper as long as this or a chapter. They are the topics of classical rhetoric. They are the channels our minds naturally run in whether we are writing a sentence or a paragraph or planning a paper. There is no point in restricting a class (as for a whole semester in a freshman course I once taught) to a single method of development until the last week, when we reached what the textbook called a "combination of methods." It is almost impossible to write a paragraph without employing a combination of methods or to find paragraphs that do not.

In another article ("Notes Toward a New Rhetoric: II. A Lesson from Hemingway," *College English*, October 1963), I maintained that in representational (or narrative-descriptive) writing, where the aim is to *picture* actions and objects, there are only three methods of development, of description, as I called them, only three things one can do to present an image. These methods

---

* In this article I propose to deal only with the paragraphs of discursive writing and to exclude from these the short introductory and transitional and concluding paragraphs.

are to point to (1) a quality or attribute or to (2) a detail or (3) to make a comparison. A single sentence may exemplify all three: "The gypsy was walking out toward the bull again, walking heel-and-toe, insultingly, like a ballroom dancer, the red shafts of the banderillos twitching with his walk"—Hemingway. These methods are exactly parallel to the methods of development or support in discursive writing. The great difference is that in representational writing the methods are so few and in discursive writing so many. In either kind of writing the methods of description or development are hard to discern except in the light of what may be called a "structural analysis."

In the light of such a structural analysis, most paragraphs are like the sentences I called "cumulative." They exemplify the four principles proposed for the rhetoric of the sentence. Let us think of the topic sentence as parallel to the base clause of a sentence and the supporting sentences as parallel to the added single-word modifiers and clusters and subordinate and relative clauses. (1) Then it is obvious that there could be no paragraphs without *addition*. (2) When a supporting sentence is added, both writer and reader must see the *direction of modification* or *direction of movement*. Discerning the direction is easier in the sentence because the sentence is self-contained and the elements added differ in form from the base clause. The direction of movement in the paragraph is explained below. The failure to see the relation of each upcoming sentence to what has gone before is probably one source of the difficulty many people have in reading. (3) When sentences are added to develop a topic or subtopic, they are usually at a lower *level of generality*—usually, but not always, because sometimes an added sentence is more general than the one it is added to. (4) Finally, the more sentences the writer adds, the denser the *texture*. The paragraphs our students write are likely to be as thin-textured as their sentences, and teachers can use this structural analysis of the paragraph to *generate* paragraphs of greater depth.

I have arranged the details of this approach to the paragraph under nine headings.

1. The paragraph may be defined as a sequence of structurally related sentences.

By a sequence of structurally related sentences I mean a group of sentences related to one another by coordination and subordination. If the first sentence of a paragraph is the topic sentence, the second is quitely likely to be a comment on it, a development of it, and therefore subordinate to it. The third sentence may be coordinate with the second sentence (as in this paragraph) or subordinate to it. The fourth sentence may be coordinate with either the second or third (or with both if they themselves are coordinate, as in this paragraph) or subordinate to the third. And so on. A sentence that is not coordinate with any sentence above it or subordinate to the next above it, breaks the sequence. The paragraph has begun to drift from its moorings, or the writer has unwittingly begun a new paragraph.

2. The top sentence of the sequence is the topic sentence.

The topic sentence is comparable to the base clause of a cumulative sentence. It is the sentence on which the others depend. It is the sentence whose assertion is supported or whose meaning is explicated or whose parts are detailed by the sentences added to it. In the examples that follow, it will always be marked 1, for the top level.

3. The topic sentence is nearly always the first sentence of the sequence.

The contrast between deductive and inductive, or between analytic and synthetic as it is sometimes put, seems to have led us to assume that the one kind of movement is as common as the other and that the topic sentence therefore is as likely to appear at the end as at the beginning. The many scores of paragraphs I have analyzed for this study do not bear out this assumption. Except as noted in point 7 below, the topic sentence occurs almost invariably at the beginning. In fact, I do not have clear-cut examples of topic sentences in the other theoretically possible positions. Readers may check their own actual practice and mine in this piece.

In connected writing, the topic sentence varies greatly in how explicit it is in designating the thesis of the paragraph. Sometimes it is quite explicit; sometimes it is a mere sign pointing to the turn the new paragraph is going to take. Sometimes it is the shortest sentence of the paragraph; sometimes it is not even a grammatically complete sentence. It seems to me that these differences are irrelevant, provided only that the reader gets the signal and the writer remembers the signal he has called.

4. Simple sequences are of two sorts—coordinate and subordinate.

Here the parallel between sentence and paragraph becomes fully evident. In analyzing the rhetoric of the sentence, I described what I called the two-level and the multilevel sentence. Here is an example of each and a paragraph exactly parallel in structure with each. The two sets of terms seem to me necessary to put the emphasis where it is needed in teaching and to avoid conflict with the use in grammar of *coordination* and *subordination.*

A. TWO-LEVEL SENTENCE

1 [Lincoln's] words still linger on the lips—
  2 eloquent and cunning, yes,
  2 vindictive and sarcastic in political debate,
  2 rippling and ribald in jokes,
  2 reverent in the half-formed utterance of prayer.

Alistair Cooke

A. COORDINATE SEQUENCE PARAGRAPH

1 This is the essence of the religious spirit—the sense of power, beauty, greatness, truth infinitely beyond one's own reach, but infinitely to be aspired to.
  2 It invests men with a pride in a purpose and with humility in accomplishment.
  2 It is the source of all true tolerance, for in its light all men see other men as they see themselves, as being capable of being more than they are, and yet falling short, inevitably, of what they can imagine human opportunities to be.
  2 It is the supporter of human dignity and pride and the dissolver of vanity.
  2 And it is the very creator of the scientific spirit; for without the aspiration to understand and control the miracle of life, no man would have sweated in a laboratory or tortured his brain in the exquisite search after truth.

Dorothy Thompson, "The Education of the Heart"

B. MULTILEVEL SENTENCE

1 A small negro girl develops from the sheet of glare-frosted walk,
  2 walking barefooted,

3 her brown legs striking and recoiling from the hot
cement,
  4 her feet curling in,
    5 only the outer edges touching.

B. SUBORDINATE SEQUENCE PARAGRAPH

1 The process of learning is essential to our lives.
  2 All higher animals seek it deliberately.
    3 They are inquisitive and they experiment.
      4 An experiment is a sort of harmless trial run of some
action which we shall have to make in the real
world; and this, whether it is made in the laboratory by scientists or by fox-cubs outside their earth.
        5 The scientist experiments and the cub plays;
both are learning to correct their errors of judgment in a setting in which errors are not fatal.
        6 Perhaps this is what gives them both their air of
happiness and freedom in these activities.

J. Bronowski, *The Common Sense of*
Science (Vintage), p. 111.

The analytical procedure for discovering the structure
is really quite simple. There is no problem in locating
the base clause of a sentence, and one can assume—
provisionally (see 6 and 7 below)—that the first sentence
of a paragraph is the topic sentence. Then, going sentence by sentence through the paragraph, one searches
in the sentences above for likenesses—that is, for evi-
dences of coordination. In both sets of two examples, the
second element is *unlike* the first one; it is different and
so it is set down as subordinate—that is, it is indented
and numbered level 2. With the third element the two
sets part company. In the examples marked A, the third
element is *like* the second, it is parallel to the second,
and so it is set down as coordinate. The clearest mark of

coordination is identity of structure at the beginning of the sentence. The fourth element is like both the second and third; and the fifth is like the second, third, and fourth. All the elements marked 2 have the same relation to one another; they are siblings. And because of this, they all have the same immediate relation to level 1, the base clause or topic sentence; they are all children of the same mother. In the examples marked B, on the other hand, the third element is *unlike* the second, and of course unlike the first; the fourth is unlike the third or any other above it, and so on. Search as you may, you will find no signs of parallelism. So, instead of two generations, there are five in the sentence and six in the paragraph. No element after the second is related immediately to level 1; it is related to it only through all of the intermediate generations.

The fact that there are two kinds of sequence makes all the difference in what we can say about the paragraph.

It should be evident how we must treat the methods of development or support. In the coordinate sequence, all the coordinate sentences employ the *same* method— in this paragraph they enumerate the *results* or *effects*. In the subordinate sequence, every added sentence may, and likely will, employ a *different* method. There is no theoretic limit to the number of levels, and the lists of methods in our textbooks are far from exhausting the whole range of what we may say in discursive writing to develop or support a topic.

It should be evident, also, that we need two separate sets of yardsticks for measuring such things as unity, coherence, and emphasis. Take coherence, for example. The repetition of structure in A is all that is necessary to join sentence to sentence at the same level. Any connectives other than the simple *and* for the last member would be an impertinence—*again, moreover, in the same vein, in addition* would be a hindrance rather than a help. But repetition of structure *is* necessary; like things in like ways is one of the imperatives of discursive writing. Any attempt to introduce variety in the sentence beginnings, by varying the pattern or by putting something before the subject, would be like trying to vary the columns of the Parthenon. In a subordinate sequence, just as clearly, repetition of structure must be avoided. Each added sentence, being different in the method of development, must be different in form. In a subordinate sequence, the problems of unity, coherence, and emphasis are altogether different—and more difficult.

Another paragraph will illustrate two other points. First, a writer sometimes intends a coordinate sequence but, like the dog that turns around once or twice before he settles down, takes, and sometimes wastes, a sentence or two before he begins his enumeration. (For other examples see paragraphs E, J, and O.) Second, the coordinate sentences need not be identical in structure; they need only be like enough for the reader to place them. In this paragraph it is evident that all three sentences at level 3 present *examples*.

C. COORDINATE SEQUENCE

1 He [the native speaker] may, of course, speak a form of English that marks him as coming from a rural or an unread group.

  2 But if he doesn't mind being so marked, there's no reason why he should change.

    3 Samuel Johnson kept a Staffordshire burr in his speech all his life.

3 In Burns's mouth the despised lowland Scots dialect served just as well as the "correct" English spoken by ten million of his southern contemporaries.

3 Lincoln's vocabulary and his way of pronouncing certain words were sneered at by many better educated people at the time, but he seemed to be able to use the English language as effectively as his critics.

Bergen Evans, *Comfortable Words*, p. 6.

5. The two sorts of sequence combine to produce the commonest sort—the mixed sequence.

Simple sequences, especially coordinate ones, are not common. More often than not, subordinate sentences are added to add depth to coordinate sequences, and coordinate sentences are added to emphasize points made in subordinate sequences. The resulting mixed sequences reveal their origin as derived from either coordinate or subordinate sequences.

My justification for the term *generative* lies here. The teacher can, with perfect naturalness, suggest the addition of subordinate sentences to clarify and of coordinate sentences to emphasize or to enumerate. With these additions the writer is not padding; he is putting himself imaginatively in the reader's place and anticipating his questions and resistances. He is learning to treat his subject home.

D. MIXED SEQUENCE—BASED ON COORDINATE SEQUENCE

1 The other [mode of thought] is the scientific method.

2 It subjects the conclusions of reason to the arbitrament of hard fact to build an increasing body of tested knowledge.

2 It refuses to ask questions that cannot be answered, and rejects such answers as cannot be provided except by Revelation.

2 It discovers the relatedness of all things in the universe—
   of the motion of the moon to the influence of the earth
   and sun, of the nature of the organism to its environ-
   ment, of human civilization to the conditions under
   which it is made.

2 It introduces history into everything.

  3 Stars and scenery have their history, alike with plant
    species or human institutions, and
    nothing is intelligible without some knowledge of its
    past.

    4 As Whitehead has said, each event is the reflection
     or effect of every other event, past as well as
     present.

2 It rejects dualism.

  3 The supernatural is in part the region of the natural
    that has not yet been understood, in part an inven-
    tion of human fantasy, in part the unknowable.

  3 Body and soul are not separate entities, but two aspects
    of one organization, and
    Man is that portion of the universal world-stuff that
    has evolved until it is capable of rational and pur-
    poseful values.

    4 His place in the universe is to continue that evolu-
    tion and to realize those values.

> Julian Huxley, *Man in the Modern
> World* (Mentor), pp. 146-47.

This paragraph suggests careful calculation of what
could be left to the reader and what must be made more
explicit. Huxley took a chance on the first two items.
What he added to the third made it a two-level sentence.
The sentences he added to the last two made the paragraph a mixed one. He was under no obligation to
expand all five items equally. The writer's guide is his
own sense of what the reader must be told. In our classes

we must work to develop this sense. The difference is often the difference between self-expression and communication.

E. MIXED SEQUENCE—BASED ON COORDINATE SEQUENCE

1 An obvious classification of meaning is that based on scope.

1 This is to say, meaning may be generalized (extended, widened) or it may be specialized (restricted, narrowed).

   2 When we increase the scope of a word, we reduce the elements of its contents.

      3 For instance *tail* (from OE *taegl*) in earlier times seems to have meant 'hairy caudal appendage, as of a horse.'

         4 When we eliminated the hairiness (or the horsiness) from the meaning, we increased its scope, so that in Modern English the word means simply 'caudal appendage.'

         4 The same thing has happened to Danish *hale,* earlier 'tail of a cow.'

            5 In course of time the cow was eliminated, and in present-day Danish the word means simply 'tail,' having undergone a semantic generalization precisely like that of the English word cited;
the closely related Icelandic *hali* still keeps the cow in the picture.

      3 Similarly, a *mill* was earlier a place for making things by the process of grinding, that is, for making meal.

         4 The words *meal* and *mill* are themselves related, as one might guess from their similarity.

            5 A mill is now simply a place for making things: the grinding has been eliminated, so that we may speak of a woolen mill, a steel mill, or even a gin mill.

      3 The word *corn* earlier meant 'grain' and is in fact related to the word *grain.*

4 It is still used in this general sense in England, as in the "Corn Laws," but

specifically it may mean either oats (for animals) or wheat (for human beings).

4 In American usage *corn* denotes maize, which is of course not at all what Keats meant in his "Ode to a Nightingale" when he described Ruth as standing "in tears amid the alien corn."

3 The building in which corn, regardless of its meaning, is stored is called a barn.

4 *Barn* earlier denoted a storehouse for barley; the word is in fact a compound of two Old English words, *bere* 'barley' and *aern* 'house.'

5 By elimination of a part of its earlier content, the scope of this word has been extended to mean a storehouse for any kind of grain.

5 American English has still further generalized by eliminating the grain, so that *barn* may mean also a place for housing livestock.

Thomas Pyles, *The Origins and Development of the English Language*, pp. 306-07.

Here the development has proceeded so far that the four coordinate sentences (level 3) have become in effect subtopic sentences. The paragraph could be subdivided, making them the topic sentences of a series of paragraphs. The long paragraph looks well on a book page; the shorter paragraphs would look more palatable in narrow newspaper columns. Either way, the effect would not be essentially different.

The problem of a reader tackling a long paragraph like this is to identify the coordinate sentences. He reads one 3rd-level sentence and then some sentences explaining it as an example of semantic generalization. He must be aware when he has come to the end of that explanation and must then shift his attention back to level 3. He must recognize the direction of movement. The first three 3rd-level sentences are easy to spot because like things have been put in like ways: the italicized words chosen as examples have been made the grammatical subject or apposed to the subject. But the opportunity to make a deft transition led the author to vary the pattern for the fourth. I have seen readers stumble at this point, and I have seen some make Danish *hale* parallel to the four English words.

F. MIXED SEQUENCE—BASED ON COORDINATE SEQUENCE

1 This is a point so frequently not understood that it needs some dwelling on.
  2 Consider how difficult it is to find a tenable argument that *thrown*, say, is intrinsically better than *throwed*.
    3 We can hardly say that the simple sound is better.
      4 For if it were, we would presumably also prefer *rown* to *rowed*, *hown* to *hoed*, *strown* to *strode*, and
      we don't.
    3 Nor can we argue convincingly that *throwed* should be avoided because it did not occur in earlier English.
      4 Many forms which occurred in earlier English cannot now be used.
        5 As we mentioned earlier, *holp* used to be the past tense form of *help*; *helped* was incorrect.
        5 But we could not now say "He holp me a good deal."
  2 As for "me and Jim," the statement that *I* should be used in the subject position begs the question.
    3 One can ask why *I* should be the subject form, and to this there is no answer.

4 As a matter of fact, *you* was at one time the object
  form of the second person
  plural, *ye* being the subject form.
4 But no one objects now to a sentence like "You
  were there."

Paul Roberts

I have included this paragraph to illustrate further
the kind of clues that mark coordination: at the first
level 3, *we can hardly say: nor can we argue*; at level 5,
used to be: now; at the second level 4, *was at one time:
now*. At level 2 there are no verbal clues; the reader just
has to recognize that "me and Jim" is another example
like "throwed" to illustrate the point that needs dwelling
on.

G. MIXED SEQUENCE—BASED ON SUBORDINATE SEQUENCE

1 The purpose of science is to describe the world in an
  orderly scheme or language which will help us to look
  ahead.
2 We want to forecast what we can of the future behaviour
  of the world;
  particularly we want to forecast how it would behave
  under several alternative actions of our own between
  which we are usually trying to choose.
3 This is a very limited purpose.
  4 It has nothing whatever to do with bold generaliza-
    tions about the universal workings of cause and
    effect.
  4 It has nothing to do with cause and effect at all, or
    with any other special mechanism.
  4 Nothing in this purpose, which is to order the world
    as an aid to decision and action, implies that the
    order must be of one kind rather than another.
    5 The order is what we find to work, conveniently
      and instructively.
    5 It is not something we stipulate;

it is not something we can dogmatise about.
It is what we find;
it is what we find useful.

J. Bronowsky, *The Common Sense of Science,*
pp. 70-71.

This would be a simple five-level sequence but for the repetition at levels 4 and 5. It is a fair guess that the desire for rhetorical emphasis generated these additions. With five statements there could be five 5th-level sentences, but the author has chosen to put them in three groups. This is a matter of paragraph punctuation (see 9 below).

H. MIXED SEQUENCE—BASED ON SUBORDINATE SEQUENCE
1 Science as we know it indeed is a creation of the last three
    hundred years.
  2 It has been made in and by the world that took its settled
      shape about 1660, when Europe at last shook off the
      long nightmare of religious wars and settled into a
      life of inquisitive trade and industry.
    3 Science is embodied in those new societies;
      it has been made by them and has helped to make
      them.
      4 The medieval world was passive and symbolic;
        it saw in the forms of nature the signatures of the
        Creator.
      4 From the first stirrings of science among the mer-
        chant adventurers of the Renaissance, the modern
        world has been an active machine.
        5 That world became the everyday world of trade
          in the seventeenth century, and
          the interests were appropriately astronomy and
          the instruments of voyage, among them the
          magnet.
        5 A hundred years later, at the Industrial Revolu-

> tion, the interest shifted to the creation and use
> of power.
>
> 6 This drive to extend the strength of man and
>   what he can do in a day's work has remained
>   our interest since.
>
> 7 In the last century it moved from steam to
>   electricity.
>
> 7 Then in 1905, in that wonderful year when
>   . . . he published papers which made
>   outstanding advances in three different
>   branches of physics, Einstein first wrote
>   down the equations which suggested that
>   matter and energy are interchangeable
>   states.
>
> 7 Fifty years later, we command a reservoir of
>   power in matter almost as large as the sun,
>   which we now realize manufactures its heat
>   for us in just this way, by the annihilation
>   of its matter.
>
> J. Bronowski, *The Common Sense of
> Science*, pp. 97-98.

Conventionally, the "movement" of this paragraph
might be called chronological; but it is only roughly so—
it leaps, and at levels 4, 5, and 7 it lingers. Note the
marks of coordination: level 4, *the medieval . . . passive:
the modern . . . active*; level 5, *the seventeenth century:
a hundred years later*; level 7, depending on *since* at
level 6, *in the last century: then in 1905: fifty years later.*
The first sentence at level 4 ("The medieval world
. . .") is interesting because the topic sentence limits
the time to "the last three hundred years." One could
easily read through levels 1-5 skipping "The medieval
world. . . ." The sentence has been inserted—extralogi-
cally and extrachronologically—in order to set up a

contrast. Such inserted sentences are fairly common and
were at first very puzzling to me. Occasionally, also, one
encounters and is puzzled by a parenthetic sentence.
Such sentences should be set off by parentheses, but all
sentences so set off are not extrasequential.

6. Some paragraphs have no top, no topic, sentence.

I. PARAGRAPH WITHOUT TOPIC SENTENCE

2 In Spain, where I saw him last, he looked profoundly
Spanish.

  3 He might have passed for one of those confidential
street dealers who earn their living selling spurious
Parker pens in the cafés of Málaga or Valencia.

    4 Like them, he wore a faded chalk-striped shirt, a
coat slung over his shoulders, a trim, dark mous-
tache, and a sleazy, fat-cat smile.

    4 His walk, like theirs, was a raffish saunter, and every-
thing about him seemed slept in, especially his
hair, a nest of small, wet serpents.

  3 Had he been in Seville and his clothes been more
formal, he could have been mistaken for a pampered
elder son idling away a legacy in dribs and on drabs,
the sort you see in windows along the Sierpes, apparently stuffed.

2 In Italy he looks Italian; in Greece, Greek:
wherever he travels on the Mediterranean coast, Tennessee Williams takes on a protective colouring which
melts him into his background, like a lizard on a rock.

2 In New York or London he seems out of place, and is
best explained away as a retired bandit.

  3 Or a beach comber: shave the beard off any of the
self-portraits Gauguin painted in Tahiti, soften the
features a little, and you have a sleepy outcast face
that might well be Tennessee's.

Kenneth Tynan, Curtains

The three sentences marked level 2 are clearly coordinate. But there is no superordinate sentence to umbrella them; that is, there is no level 1, no topic sentence. With paragraphs such as this the topic can usually be inferred from the preceding paragraph. But sometimes the topic sentence is actually part of the preceding paragraph, arbitrarily and illogically separated. Or, as in J, the preceding paragraph *is* the topic sentence; the two paragraphs of J constitute a single sequence. The basic pattern here is like that of B; but with the series of three examples disjoined, they stand alone in a paragraph that has no topic sentence.

J. TOPIC SENTENCE IN PRECEDING PARAGRAPH

1 The mystical artist always sees patterns.

 2 The symbol, never quite real, tends to be expressed less and less realistically, and

  as the reality becomes abstracted the pattern comes forward.

  ¶3 The wings on Blake's angels do not look like real wings,

   nor are they there because wings belong to angels.

   4 They have been flattened, stylized, to provide a curving pointed frame, the setting required by the pattern of the composition.

  3 In Hindoo art and its branches, stylization reaches its height.

   4 Human figures are stylized far beyond the point of becoming a type;

   they too are made into patterns, schematic designs of the human body, an abstraction of humanity.

  3 In the case of an Eastern rug all desire to express any semblance of reality has gone.

   4 Such a work of art is pure decoration.

   5 It is the expression of the artist's final withdrawal

> from the visible world, essentially his denial of
> the intellect.
>
> Edith Hamilton, *The Greek Way* (Mentor),
> p. 33.

7. Some paragraphs have sentences at the beginning or at the end that do not belong to the sequence.

Occasionally a paragraph has one or more introductory (I) or transitional (T) sentences before the sequence begins. And occasionally one has a sentence or more added after the sequence has run its course; that is, the first of such sentences is not coordinate with any sentence above it or subordinate to the one next above it. They are related to the sequence, but are not a part of it; they form a conclusion (C) or a transition (T). To save space, I have quoted only enough to establish that the sentences so marked are extrasequential.

K. PARAGRAPH WITH INTRODUCTION

I1 If you are at the beach, and you take an old, dull, brown penny and rub it hard for a minute or two with handfuls of wet sand (dry sand is no good), the penny will come out a bright gold color, looking as clean and new as the day it was minted.

1 Now poetry has the same effect on words as wet sand on pennies.

  2 In what seems an almost miraculous way, it brightens up words that looked dull and ordinary.

    3 . . .

> C. Day Lewis, *Poetry for You*, pp. 8-9.

Most of the examples of what I would call introductory sentences are like this in offering a comparison. The comparison is not carried through the paragraph, but is used only as a starter.

L. PARAGRAPH WITH TRANSITION

T1 So far I've been talking about some of the world-shapes
out of which poetry is built.

　T2 But images, metaphors, and similes are not the only
things which may go to make the pattern of a poem.
1 There are meter and rhyme.
　2 You may be surprised that I have not put meter first . . .
　　　　　C. Day Lewis, *Poetry for You*, p. 33.

Transitions from paragraph to paragraph are ordinarily embedded in the topic sentence, as a single word
or a phrase, a subordinate clause, or the first part of a
compound sentence. But sometimes, as here, they take
a full sentence or more.

The first sentence of a paragraph may even be a major
transition. It may be the topic sentence of a series of
paragraphs or even the thesis sentence of an article.

M. PARAGRAPH WITH CONCLUSION

1 When we follow the growth of science, we come to understand how that movement has been probing for these
unifying concepts.
　2 Look at the movement of biology since the days of Ray
and Linnaeus: . . .
　2 Look at chemistry, from Dalton's law. . . .
　2 Look at the march of physics to unity: . . .
　　3 We have seen this lead to the creation of energy from
matter; to a picture of space as closed but possibly
expanding; and now . . . .
C1 Science is a process of creating new concepts which unify
our understanding of the world, and
　the process is today bolder and more far-reaching, more
triumphant even than at the great threshold of the
Scientific Revolution.
　　　　J. Bronowski, *The Common Sense of Science*,
　　　　　　　　pp. 132-33.

Concluding sentences are rather rare, and some of them, like this one, round off a sequence of paragraphs rather than the one they are joined to. Such concluding sentences are ordinarily at a higher level of generalization than the sentences they follow, and those who take the most general sentence to be the topic sentence may take them for topic sentences. They may say that the paragraph has two topic sentences, fore and aft.

8. Some paragraphing is illogical.

N.

1 Rhymes, as you know, generally come at the end of lines.
  2 They are put there because it helps to create and make clear the musical pattern of the stanza:
    the ear learns to expect a rhyme, just as it expects a beat, at certain definite intervals, and
    it's pleased when it finds one there.
1 But you may get a rhyme in the middle of a line, too: and some poets are extremely skilful in making assonances and other sound-echoes all over the poem.
  2 This is often done by the use of alliteration.
    3 For example,
      I hear lake water lapping with low sounds by the shore.
      ¶4 Those three 'l's' make a pleasant liquid sound:
        the sound here, in fact corresponds with the sense.
    4 So it does in
      Dry clashed his armour in the icy caves,
      where the hard 'c' of 'clashed' and 'caves' seems to dry one's mouth up when one speaks the line aloud.
                                C. Day Lewis, *Poetry for You*, pp. 35-36.

The two sentences marked 1 are clearly coordinate. One has to say, then, that the paragraph is compound (a reasonable solution; there are such paragraphs), or that the first two sentences are introductory or transitional, or that the paragraphing is simply illogical, breaking up a short sequence.

Paragraphing at level 4 is even more illogical. It breaks up a sequence at the most unexpected point. Perhaps the tired teacher will sigh "If gold rusts. . . ."

On the other hand, many a run of four or five paragraphs totaling 500-600 words can be analyzed as a single sequence, with the paragraph divisions coming logically at the subtopic sentences. This is the consummation we should work for.

9. Punctuation should be by the paragraph, not by the sentence.

o.

1 This brings me to the third failing of eighteenth century science, which I find most interesting.

2 A science which orders its thought too early is stifled.

3 For example, the ideas of the Epicureans about atoms two thousand years ago were quite reasonable; but they did only harm to a physics which could not measure temperature and pressure and learn the simpler laws which relate them.

3 Or again, the hope of the medieval alchemists that the elements might be changed was not as fanciful as we once thought.

4 But it was merely damaging to a chemistry which did not yet understand the composition of water and common salt.

J. Bronowski, The Common Sense of Science,
p. 47.

This is a minor example of punctuating without an eye to the paragraph as a whole. The two sets at level 3 are the same in intent and, except for the punctuation, the same in form. Likes have been put in unlike ways.

Paragraph punctuation usually involves the choice of whether to make compound sentences or not. In paragraph G the same author wisely grouped five coordinate statements into three sentences, sorting them out on the basis of content. Paragraph E does not really have two topic sentences, and a semicolon would avoid that appearance. I have taken it as a rule that a sentence that merely restates another is on the same level with it. If this is a bad rule, then all the numbers for level should be raised one. In paragraph P the effects of repetition and balance would be obscured if the sentences were not punctuated as compound.

P.

1 Nowhere, at no time, have there been five and a half years so alternately wondrous, compelling, swift and cruel.

  2 As the Sixties began, our aspirant astronauts had yet to enter space;

    now, they practice giant steps to the moon.

  2 Then, jet travel was a conversation piece;

    now, we change the flight if we've seen the movie.

  2 Then, we were about to be swamped by a recessionary wave;

    now, riding history's highest flood of prosperity, we are revising our assumptions about the inevitability of ebbs in our economic life.

  2 Then, our Negroes were still marshaling their forces;

    now, they have marshaled the conscience of mankind.

  2 Then, we were arguing over the fitness of a Roman Catholic to be President;

    now, we subdue the nightmare of his murder.

  2 Then, a Southerner in the White House seemed politically unthinkable;

now, a Southerner builds with the most emphatic man-
date we have ever bestowed.

2 Then, John Birch was an unknown soldier, actresses still
wore clothes at work, and dancing was something a
man and woman did together.

Leonard Gross, *Look*, 6/29/65

❋   ❋   ❋

Is the paragraph a logical entity, a sequence of structurally related sentences, or is it a visual unit, with the
first line indented and the last line left incomplete?
Clearly it is both and the two jostle; sequences are
broken up because writers don't recognize them or because they want their paragraphs to look all of a size.
This lack of "register" between the logical and the visual
has kept us from making sense of the paragraphs we encounter in our reading. The problem is the same as that
of sentences that are fragmentary or run together. These
atypical units do not compel us to deny or disregard
grammatical relations or to assert that the sentence is a
myth.

I'd like to claim that the paragraph that submits to
this kind of structural analysis is thereby a good paragraph and the only good paragraph. But I only claim
that the structural relations I have disclosed are real
(they were discovered by induction), and I urge my
readers to discover them for themselves. The teacher
who thinks that writing is an art and that art cannot be
taught, that the teacher can only inspire and then keep
out of the way, will not find anything he can use. But
the teacher who believes, as I do, that the only freedom
in any art comes from the mastery of technique, may
find here the means both to kindle and restrain.

Generative Grammars and the Concept of Literary Style

RICHARD OHMANN

Richard Ohmann (1931-   ) was born in Ohio and educated at Oberlin College and Harvard University, where he was a junior fellow. Since 1961, he has taught at Wesleyan University (Connecticut), where he is now associate professor of English. In 1966, he became editor of *College English,* one of the journals of the National Council of Teachers of English. Among his works are *Shaw: The Style and the Man* (1962) and, with Harold Martin, *The Logic and Rhetoric of Exposition* (rev. ed., 1963). Like Young and Becker, Milic, and Sledd, Ohmann believes that linguistic theory can provide a basis for rhetorical theory: that the transformational grammatical theory of Noam Chomsky can provide a basis for a theory of style, one of the five categories of classical rhetoric. Just as Steinmann finds the concept of choice among synonymous expressions central to rhetoric in general, Ohmann, like Milic and Sledd, finds it central to stylistics in particular; and transformational grammatical theory, he believes, provides formal criteria for synonymy. Only such a theory, he says, "is powerful enough to set forth, formally and accurately, stylistic *alternatives* to a given passage or a given set of linguistic habits."

A style is a way of writing—that is what the word means. And that is almost as much as one can say with assurance on the subject, which has been remarkably unencumbered by theoretical insights. Yet we know a good deal more than that, in a way: the same way, roughly in which a native speaker "knows" the grammar of English, although no existing grammatical analysis gives a full and adequate account of his linguistic intuition. Readers familiar with literature have what might sensibly be called a *stylistic* intuition, a rather loosely structured, but often reliable, feeling for the quiddity of a writer's linguistic method, a sense of differences between stretches of literary discourse which are not differences in content. In fact many readers can tell, by skimming a batch of unfamiliar passages, not only that the differences are there, but who the authors are. Read the first few paragraphs of a *New Yorker* story and you can often (without a surreptitious glance at the end) identify it as a Cheever, an O'Hara, an Updike, or a Salinger, even if the subject matter is uncharacteristic. Further evidence, if any is needed, of the reliability of stylistic intuitions is the ability of some to write convincing parodies, and of others to recognize them as such. Thus the theorist of style is confronted by a kind of task that is commonplace enough in most fields: the task of explicating and toughening up for rigorous use a notion already familiar to the layman.

But in stylistics the scholar has always had to make do with a theoretical apparatus not far removed from that

This paper is a preliminary version of a chapter from Professor Ohmann's planned book on the subject, to be published by the Oxford University Press, New York, tentatively in 1968.

From *Word*, XX (December, 1964), 423-439. Reprinted by permission of *Word* and the author.

of the layman. And although many practitioners have plied their craft with great subtlety, a survey of their work leaves one far from certain what that craft *is*. For the attempt to isolate the cues one attends to in identifying styles and in writing stylistic parody has sprawled out into an almost embarrassing profusion of critical methods. And most of these methods, I believe, are interesting in inverse proportion to their emphasis on what we sense as style. The following list will suggest, but not exhaust, the multiplicity of approaches:

(1) What might be called "diachronic stylistics," the study of changes in national literary style from one period to the next. Clearly this approach presupposes a mastery of what might be called

(2) "Synchronic stylistics," or the study of this or that period style. Since the style of a period can only be the sum of linguistic habits shared by most writers of that period, synchronic stylistics presupposes in turn the ability to describe the style of a single writer. But there is little agreement upon how such description is to be managed; many methods compete for critical attention.

(3) Impressionism: the application of metaphorical labels to styles ("masculine," "limber," "staccato," "flowing," "involuted," etc.), and the attempt to evaluate (Swift's style is the best, or the most natural to English). This sort of criticism makes agreeable parlor conversation, records something of the critic's emotional response, and gives intuition its due, but little else can be said in its favor.

(4) The study of sound, especially of rhythm. This approach is capable of some rigor, but the more rigor (that is, the more strictly the critic attends to physical or to phonemic features), the less relevance to what we sense as style. For—let me state this dogmatically—in

prose, at least, rhythm as perceived is largely dependent upon syntax, and even upon content, not upon stress, intonation, and juncture alone.

(5) The study of tropes. Attention to metaphor, antithesis, synecdoche, zeugma, and the other figures of classical rhetoric often proceeds from a desire to see the writer's style in terms of what he thought he was doing, and to this extent points away from a descriptive analysis of style, and toward the history or philosophy of rhetorical theory. Even when the studies of figurative language maintain a descriptive focus, they embrace only a small, though important, part of style, and liberally mixed with content, at that.

(6) The study of imagery. The fact that a writer favors images of disease, money, battle, or the like, is frequently of great interest, but imagery divorced from its syntactic embodiment is surely more a matter of content than of style.

(7) The study of what is variously called "tone," "stance," "role," and so on: roughly, the writer's attitude toward what he is saying, toward his reader, and toward himself, as suggested by his language. The critic in this vein infers, from the locutions on the printed page, a hypothetical live situation in which such language would be appropriate, and discusses the social and emotional features of that situation. This approach has unquestionably been fruitful. Its success depends on a highly developed sense of connotative meaning, both of words and of constructions, and this sense is something that many critics possess in abundance. Tone, however, like figurative language, is only a part of style, and the question remains in what measure tone itself is a product of formal linguistic features.

(8) The study of literary structure, which, like the

study of tropes and tone, has flourished among the new critics. And to be sure, patterns of organization in a literary work are *related* to style (the way a novel is put together may have an analogue in the way a sentence is put together), but to consider structure a *component* of style, except perhaps in a short poem, stretches the meaning of the term "style" to its limits.

(9) The analysis of particular and local effects—a change of verb tense, or the placement of an interrogative, for instance, in a certain passage. Clearly, individual strategies of this sort fit more comfortably under the heading of *technique* than of style, for style has to do primarily with the habitual, the recurrent.

(10) The study of special idiosyncrasies, such as the omission of causal connectives from contexts where they usually appear. Such quirks are doubtless stylistic elements, and they can richly reward analysis, as a number of studies by Leo Spitzer have shown. But a few idiosyncrasies do not add up to a style, by any method of calculation.

(11) The study of a writer's lexicon, as pursued, for example, by Josephine Miles. Lexical preferences, unless seen in the context of a ramified system of word classes, are like imagery patterns, in that they reveal more about content than about style.

(12) The statistical study of grammatical features— abstract nouns, adjectives, subordinate clauses, questions, and the like. This method is without doubt pertinent, but significant results have been highly elusive. One reason is the crudeness of the categories which traditional grammar has made available to critics, whose knowledge of linguistics generally seems to lag by a few decades. (Linguists, by and large, have not busied them-

selves with stylistics.) Another reason, equally important, is the overwhelming inefficiency of the procedure,
given the very large number of grammatical categories,
and the lack of any grammatical system that relates them
in meaningful, formally motivated ways. Without such
a theory, a collection of counts is simply a collection of
counts.

And indeed, the inability of these and other methods,
in spite of many partial successes, to yield a full and
convincing explication of the notion of style seems in
general to follow from the absence of an appropriate
underlying linguistic and semantic theory. A style is a
characteristic use of language, and it is difficult to see
how the *uses* of a system can be understood unless the
system itself has been mapped out. It is no surprise, in
other words, to find stylistics in a state of disorganization
when syntax and semantics, upon which stylistics clearly
depends, have themselves been hampered by the lack
of a theory that is inclusive, unified, and plausible.

The situation in stylistics is understandably analogous
to that in the philosophy of language,[1] though more
muddled still. Just as philosophers have tended to con-
centrate on this or that discrete feature of language—
words, or groups of words, or grammatical predication,
or the relation of reference, or logical structure—in isolation from the rest, so analysts of style have talked about
sound, tropes, images, diction, devices of conjunction,
parallel structure, and so on, without any apparent sense
of priority or centrality among these concerns. Thus, in
a time when linguistic theory and practice have passed
through at least one renaissance, the most serviceable

---

[1] See Jerrold Katz and Jerry Fodor, "What's Wrong with the Philosophy of Language?," *Inquiry* V (1962), pp. 197–237.

studies of style[2] continue to proceed from the critic's naked intuition, fortified against the winds of ignorance only by literary sophistication and the tattered garments of traditional grammar. Especially damaging is the critic's inability, for lack of a theory, to take into account the deeper structural features of language, precisely those which should enter most revealingly into a stylistic description.

It is my contention that recent developments in generative grammar, particularly on the transformational model, promise, first, to clear away a good deal of the mist from stylistic theory, and, second, to make possible a corresponding refinement in the practice of stylistic analysis. In the remainder of this paper I hope to state a case for the first of these claims, and to make a very modest initial thrust toward documenting the second.

That Chomsky's formulation of grammatical theory is potentially useful should become apparent from an examination of the common sense notion of style. In general that notion applies to human action that is partly invariant and partly variable. A style is a *way* of doing *it*. Now this picture leads to few complications if the action is playing the piano or playing tennis. The pianist performing a Mozart concerto must strike certain notes in a certain order, under certain restrictions of tempo, in a certain relation to the orchestra, and so on. These limitations define the part of his behavior that is fixed. Likewise, the tennis player must hit the ball over the net with the racket in a way partly determined by the rules of the game (errors and cheating are not style). But each has

[2] William K. Wimsatt, *The Prose Style of Samuel Johnson* (New Haven, 1941), and Jonas Barish, *Ben Jonson and the Language of Prose Comedy* (Cambridge, Mass., 1960), to name just two of the best.

a significant amount of freedom, beyond these established regularities: the tennis player, for instance,
chooses from a repertory of strokes, shots, and possible
placements (analogous, perhaps, to the linguistic resources of the writer or speaker), and he also has freedom of intensity, smoothness, flamboyance, etc. (as the
writer or speaker has freedom in the use of paralinguistic
resources like loudness and emphatic punctuation). The
tennis player's use of these options, in so far as it is
habitual or recurrent, constitutes his style. But the relevant division between fixed and variable components in
literature is by no means so obvious. What *is* content,
and what is form, or style? The attack on a dichotomy
of form and content has been persistent in modern criticism; to change so much as a word, the argument runs,
is to change the meaning as well. This austere doctrine
has a certain theoretical appeal, given the supposed impossibility of finding exact synonyms, and the ontological
queerness of disembodied content—propositions, for instance—divorced from any verbal expression. Yet at the
same time this doctrine leads to the altogether counter-
intuitive conclusion that there can be no such thing as
style, or that style is simply a part of content.[3]

To put the problem more concretely, the idea of style
implies that words on a page might have been different,
or differently arranged, without a corresponding difference in substance. Another writer would have said *it*
another *way*. For the idea of style to apply, in short,
writing must involve choices of verbal formulation. Yet

[3] For an earlier attempt by the present author to deal with this prob-
lem, see "Prolegomena to the Analysis of Prose Style," in *Style in Prose
Fiction; English Institute Essays*, 1958, ed. Harold C. Martin (New
York, 1959), pp. 1–24.

suppose we try to list the alternatives to a given segment of prose: "After dinner, the senator made a speech." A dozen close approximations may suggest themselves ("When dinner was over, the senator made a speech," "The senator made a speech after dinner," "A speech was made by the senator after dinner," etc.), as well as a very large number of more distant renderings ("The senator made a postprandial oration," "The termination of dinner brought a speech from the senator," etc.). Which ones represent stylistic variations on the original, and which ones say different things? We may have intuitions, but to support them is no trivial undertaking. Clearly it would help to have a grammar that provided certain relationships, formally statable, of alternativeness among constructions. One such relationship, for example, might be that which holds between two different constructions that are derived from the same starting point. And, of course, a generative grammar allows the formulation of precisely this sort of relationship.

In the phrase structure component, to begin with, there are alternate ways of proceeding from identically labeled nodes, alternate ways of expanding (or rewriting) a symbol. A verb phrase may be expanded[4] into a transitive verb plus a noun phrase, a copula plus an adjective, a copula plus a noun phrase, or any one of several other combinations.[5] The various possibilities for

---

[4] I do not mean to suggest that a speaker or writer actually performs these operations. But the different possibilities of expansion in the grammar do offer an analogue to the choices open to the writer.

[5] Possibly some other order of expansion is preferable, such as the one Lees uses: VP → (Prev) Aux + MV. See Robert B. Lees, *The Grammar of English Nominalizations*, Part II, *International Journal of American Linguistics* XXVI 3 (1960), 5. If the grammar takes this form, then the choice I am speaking of enters only with the expansion of the main verb. Such questions are immaterial, however, to my point.

rewriting at this stage of the grammar account for some of the major sentence types in English, and since the structural meaning of, say, $V_t + NP$ differs considerably from that of $Be + Adj$, a writer's preference for one or another of these forms may be a stylistic choice of some interest.

But notice that the possibility of alternative routings in the phrase structure component does not really solve the problem of style in a satisfactory way. I have been looking for linguistically constant features that may be expressed in different ways. The difficulty with taking a unit like the verb phrase for such a constant is its abstractness, its lack of structure. The symbol VP merely stands for a *position* in a string at one level of description. Two different expansions of VP will both occupy the same position, but will not necessarily retain any structural feature in common. Nor will the sentences that ultimately result from the two derivations necessarily share any morphemes or even morphemes from the same classes. Thus, the rewriting of VP as $V_t + NP$ is part of a derivation that leads eventually to the sentence "Columbus discovered America," among others. But there is no kernel sentence corresponding (semantically) to this one which results from a derivation in which NP is rewritten $Be + Adj$. Sentences like "Columbus was brave," or possibly "Columbus was nautical" are about as close as one can come. And certainly they are not stylistically different expressions of the same thing, in the sense required for stylistics—not in the way that "America was discovered by Columbus" is. The phrase structure part of the grammar does not account for intuitively felt relationships of sameness and difference between sentences, for the possibility of saying one "thing" in two different ways. Perhaps this is one reason why almost no important work in stylistic criticism has evolved from the grammatical analyses of American linguists.

To be of genuine interest for stylistics, a grammar must do more than simply provide for alternate derivations from the same point of origin. There are at least three important characteristics of transformational rules which make them more promising as a source of insight into style than phrase structure rules. In the first place, a large number of transformations are optional, and in quite a different sense from the sense in which it is optional how VP is expanded. VP must *be* expanded by one of the various rules, or of course no sentence will result from the derivation. But an optional transformation need not be applied at all. Given a string or pair of strings so structured that a certain optional transformation can apply, failure to apply it will not keep the derivation from terminating in a sentence.[6] Thus "Dickens wrote *Bleak House*" is a sentence, as well as "*Bleak House* was written by Dickens," which has undergone the passive transformation. Likewise, "Dickens was the writer of *Bleak House*" is a sentence, one that comes from the same kernel string as the other two, via a different optional transformation: agentive nominalization.[7] Technically, transformations apply to underlying strings with certain structures, but for the purposes of this paper they may be thought of as manipulations— reordering, combination, addition, deletion—performed

---

[6] This is simply to rephrase the definition of an optional transformation; see Noam Chomsky, *Syntactic Structures* ('s-Gravenhage, 1957), p. 45.

[7] Lees, *op. cit.*, p. 70 (transformation T47).

on fully formed sentences, rather than as ways of *getting* to parts of fully formed sentences from incomplete, abstract symbols such as NP. Each application of a different optional transformation to a sentence results in a new sentence, similar in some ways to the original one. Thus a grammar with transformational rules will generate many pairs and limited sets of sentences, like the set of three sentences about Dickens, which belong together in an intimate structural way—not simply by virtue of being sentences. Many such sets of sentences will strike a speaker as saying "the same thing"—as being alternatives, that is, in precisely the sense required for stylistics.

A second and related reason why transformational happenings are relevant to style is the very fact that a transformation applies to one or more *strings*, or elements with structure, not to single symbols like VP, and that it applies to those strings by virtue of their structure. A transformation works changes on structure, but normally leaves *part* of the structure unchanged. And in any case, the new structure bears a precisely specifiable relationship to the old one, a relationship, incidentally, that speakers of the language will intuitively feel. Moreover, the transform retains at least some morphemes from the original string; that is, transformations are specified in such a way that "Columbus discovered America" cannot become, under the passive transformation, "*Bleak House* was written by Dickens," although this sentence has the same structure as the proper transform "America was discovered by Columbus." This property of transformations—their preserving some features from the original string—accounts for the fact that sets of sentences which are transformational alternatives

seem to be different renderings of the same proposition.[8]
Again, this is the sort of relationship which seems intuitively to underlie the notion of style, and for which only
a transformational grammar offers a formal analogue.

The third value of a transformational grammar to the
analyst of style is its power to explain how complex sentences are generated, and how they are related to simple
sentences. Writers differ noticeably in the amounts and
kinds of syntactic complexity they habitually allow
themselves, but these matters have been hard to approach through conventional methods of analysis. Since
the complexity of a sentence is the product of the generalized transformations it has gone through, a break-
down of the sentence into its component simple sentences and the generalized transformations applied (in
the order of application) will be an account of its complexity.[9] And since the same set of simple sentences may
usually be combined in different ways, a set of complex
sentences may be generated from them, each of which
differs from the others only in transformational history,
while embodying the same simple "propositions." Such
differences should be interestingly approachable through
transformational analysis. So should major variations in

[8] Notice that many such sets, including the three sentences about
Dickens, will share the same *truth conditions,* to use the philosopher's
term. This fact gives further encouragement to anyone who would treat
transformational alternatives as different expressions of the same proposition.

[9] Since deletions and additions will probably have taken place in the
course of the derivation, the complex sentence will naturally not contain
all and only all of the linguistic elements contained in the component
sentences. These must be reconstructed and supplied with appropriate
hypothetical elements, but there is generally a strong formal motivation
for reconstructing the component sentences in one way rather than another.

type of compounding: self-embedding as against left-
and right-branching, for example, or the formation of
endocentric as against the formation of exocentric constructions. These deep grammatical possibilities in a language may well be exploited differently from writer to
writer, and if so, the differences will certainly be of
stylistic interest.

Let me summarize. A generative grammar with a
transformational component provides apparatus for
breaking down a sentence in a stretch of discourse into
underlying kernel sentences (or strings, strictly speaking) and for specifying the grammatical operations that
have been performed upon them. It also permits the
analyst to construct, from the same set of kernel sentences, other non-kernel sentences. These may reasonably be thought of as *alternatives* to the original
sentence, in that they are simply different constructs out
of the identical elementary grammatical units.[10] Thus
the idea of alternative phrasings, which is crucial to the
notion of style, has a clear analogue within the framework of a transformational grammar.

But is it the *right* analogue? What I have called
"transformational alternatives" are different derivatives
from the same kernel sentences. The notion of style calls
for different ways of expressing the same content. Kernel
sentences are not "content," to be sure. Yet they *have*
content, and much of that content is preserved through
transformational operations. "Dickens was the writer of

[10] Of course the alternative forms need not be complete sentences, or
single sentences. That is, the alternatives to sentence A may include
(1) sentence B, (2) part of sentence C, and (3) the group of sentences,
D, E, and F. The most interesting alternatives to a given sentence often
arrange the kernel material in units of different lengths.

Bleak House and America was discovered by Columbus"
says much the same thing, if not exactly the same thing,
as "Dickens wrote *Bleak House*; Columbus discovered
America." Of course some transformations import new
content, others eliminate features of content, and no
transformation leaves content absolutely unaltered. The
analogue is not perfect. But it is worth remembering that
other kinds of tampering with sentences (e.g., substitu-
tion of synonyms) also change content. And, to look at
it another way, the most useful sense of "content"—
cognitive content—may be such that transformations do
generally leave it unaltered (and such that synonyms do
exist).[11] In any case, transformational alternatives come
as close to "different expressions of the same content" as
other sorts of alternatives; moreover, they have the practical advantage of being accessible to formal, rather than
to impressionistic, analysis. There is at least some reason,
then, to hold that a style is in part a characteristic way of
deploying the transformational apparatus of a language,
and to expect that transformational analysis will be a
valuable aid to the description of actual styles.

So much for theory and prophecy. The final proof
must come, if it comes at all, from a fairly extensive
attempt to study literary styles in the way I am suggest-
ing. For a transformational analysis, however appealing
theoretically, will not be worth much unless it can im-
plement better stylistic descriptions than have been
achieved by other methods—"better" in that they isolate
more fully, economically, and demonstrably the linguistic features to which a perceptive reader responds in
sensing one style to be different from another. The space

[11] I owe this point and several others to correspondence and conversation with Noam Chomsky.

available here will not suffice for a full scale demonstration, nor do I now have at my disposal nearly enough stylistic description to prove my case. Besides, the necessary grammatical machinery is by no means available yet (in fact, it is too early to say with certainty that Chomsky's plan for grammars is the right one—there are many dissenters). I shall use the rest of this paper merely to outline, by example, a simple analytic procedure that draws on the concept of grammatical transformations, and to suggest some virtues of this procedure.

My first specimen passage comes from Faulkner's story, "The Bear." It is part of a sentence nearly two pages long, and its style is complex, highly individual, and difficult—if it is read aloud, most hearers will not grasp it on first hearing. It is also, I believe, quite typically Faulknerian:

the desk and the shelf above it on which rested the ledgers in which McCaslin recorded the slow outward trickle of food and supplies and equipment which returned each fall as cotton made and ginned and sold (two threads frail as truth and impalpable as equators yet cable-strong to bind for life them who made the cotton to the land their sweat fell on), and the older ledgers clumsy and archaic in size and shape, on the yellowed pages of which were recorded in the faded hand of his father Theophilus and his uncle Amodeus during the two decades before the Civil War, the manumission in title at least of Carothers McCaslin's slaves: . . .[12]

I propose to reduce the complexity of the passage by reversing the effects of three generalized transformations, plus a few related singular transformations:

(1) The relative clause transformation (GT19 in Lees'

[12] William Faulkner, "The Bear," in *Go Down Moses* (New York: Modern Library, 1942), pp. 255–256.

The Grammar of English Nominalizations, p. 89), along with the wh-transformations (Lees, T5 and T6, p. 39), the transformation which later deletes "which" and "be" to leave post-nominal modifiers (Lees, T58, p. 94), and the transformation which shifts these modifiers to pre-nominal position (Lees, T64, p. 98).[13]

(2) The conjunction transformation (Chomsky, *Syntactic Structures,* p. 36).

(3) The comparative transformation, which, along with several reduction transformations and one order change,[14] is responsible for sentences like "George is as tall as John."[15]

Without this grammatical apparatus, the passage reads as follows:

the desk. The shelf was above it. The ledgers$_1$ rested on the shelf. The ledgers$_1$ were old. McCaslin recorded the trickle of food in the ledgers$_1$. McCaslin recorded the trickle of supplies in the ledgers$_1$. McCaslin recorded the trickle of equipment in the ledgers$_1$. The trickle was slow. The trickle was outward. The trickle returned each fall as cotton. The cotton was made. The cotton was ginned. The cotton was sold. The trickle was a thread. The cotton was a thread. The threads were frail. Truth is frail. The threads were impalpable. Equators are impalpable. The threads were strong to bind them for life to the land. They made the cotton. Their sweat fell on the land. Cables are strong. The ledgers$_2$ were old. The

---

[13] For another version of these transformations, see Carlota S. Smith, "A Class of Complex Modifiers in English," *Language* XXXVII (1961), pp. 347–348, 361–362.

[14] Strong as cable → cable-strong.

[15] Lees, "Grammatical Analysis of the English Comparative Construction," *Word* XVII (1961), pp. 182–183. Carlota S. Smith, in "A Class of Complex Modifiers in English," offers a fuller treatment of such constructions, but Lees' simpler analysis is adequate for my present purposes.

ledgers$_2$ rested on the shelf. The ledgers$_2$ were clumsy in size. The ledgers$_2$ were clumsy in shape. The ledgers$_2$ were archaic in size. The ledgers$_2$ were archaic in shape. On the pages of the ledgers$_2$ were recorded in the hand of his father during the two decades the manumission in title at least of Carothers McCaslin's slaves. On the pages of the ledgers$_2$ were recorded in the hand of his uncle during the two decades the manumission in title at least of Carothers McCaslin's slaves. The pages were yellowed. The hand was faded. The decades were before the Civil War. His father was Theophilus. His uncle was Amodeus.[16]

There is some artificiality in this process, of course. The order of the reduced sentences is in part arbitrary. More important, the transformations I have reversed are not the last ones applied in the generation of the original construction; hence precisely the set of sentences (strings) above would not have occurred at any point in the derivation. Nonetheless, this drastic reduction of the original passage reveals several important things:

(1) The content of the passage remains roughly the same: aside from the loss of distinctions between "and" and "yet," "as —— as" and "more —— than," relative clauses and conjoined sentences, and the like, changes in content are minor. But the style, obviously, has undergone a revolution. In the reduced form of the passage there are virtually no traces of what we recognize as Faulkner's style.

(2) This denaturing has been accomplished by reversing the effects of only three generalized transformations, as well as a few related singular transformations. The total number of optional transformations involved is negligible as against the total number that apparently

---

[16] Subscripts mark differences in referent.

exist in the grammar as a whole. In other words, the style of the original passage leans heavily upon a very small amount of grammatical apparatus.

(3) Most of the sentences in the reduced version of the passage are kernel sentences. Most of the rest are only one transformation away from kernel sentences. Further reduction, by undoing any number of other transformations, would not change the passage or its style nearly so much as has already been done.[17]

(4) The three major transformations I have deleted have an important feature in common. Each of them combines two sentences that share at least one morpheme,[18] and in such a way that the transform may contain only one occurrence of that morpheme (or those morphemes), while preserving the unshared parts of the original sentences. That is to say, these transformations are all what might be called "additive." To put the matter semantically, they offer methods of adding information about a single "thing" with a minimum of repetition. Thus the two sentences "The threads were impalpable" and "The threads were frail" might be combined through any one of the three generalized transformations at issue here: "The threads which were impalpable were frail" (relative); "The threads were frail and impalpable" (conjunction); and "The threads were more frail than impalpable" (comparison). The three transforms are somewhat similar, both formally and semantically; and it seems reasonable to suppose that a writer whose style is so largely based on just these

[17] Passives and pronouns are also fairly prominent here, but not enough to make them striking as stylistic features.
[18] Except that conjunction may also operate on two sentences with no common morphemes.

three semantically related transformations demonstrates in that style a certain conceptual orientation, a preferred way of organizing experience.[19] If that orientation could be specified, it would almost certainly provide insight into other, non-stylistic features of Faulkner's thought and artistry. The possibility of such insight is one of the main justifications for studying style.

The move from formal description of styles to critical and semantic interpretation should be the ultimate goal of stylistics, but in this article I am concerned only with the first step: description. My first example shows that the style of at least one short passage can be rather efficiently and informatively described in terms of a few grammatical operations. It might be objected, however, that the transformations I have concentrated on in destroying the style of the Faulkner passage are of such prominence in the grammar, and in the use of English, that *any* writer must depend heavily upon them. To show that this is not universally the case, it is sufficient to perform the same reductions on a characteristic passage from the work of another writer with a quite different style. Consider, therefore, the conclusion of Hemingway's story, "Soldier's Home":

So his mother prayed for him and then they stood up and Krebs kissed his mother and went out of the house. He had tried so to keep his life from being complicated. Still, none of it had touched him. He had felt sorry for his mother and she had made him lie. He would go to Kansas City and get a job and she would feel all right about it. There would be

[19] It is apparently common for stylistic features to cluster like this in the work of an author. See my study, *Shaw; The Style and the Man* (Middletown, Conn., 1962), for numerous examples, and for an attempt to link style with cognitive orientation.

one more scene maybe before he got away. He would not go down to his father's office. He would miss that one. He wanted his life to go smoothly. It had just gotten going that way. Well, that was all over now, anyway. He would go over to the schoolyard and watch Helen play indoor baseball.[20]

Reversing the effects of the relative and comparative transformations barely alters the passage: only the prenominal modifier "indoor" is affected. Removing the conjunctions does result in some changes:

So his mother prayed for him. Then they stood up. Krebs kissed his mother. Krebs went out of the house. He had tried so to keep his life from being complicated. Still, none of it had touched him. He had felt sorry for his mother. She had made him lie. He would go to Kansas City. He would get a job. She would feel all right about it. There would be one more scene maybe before he got away. He would not go down to his father's office. He would miss that one. He wanted his life to go smoothly. It had just gotten going that way. Well, that was all over now, anyway. He would go over to the schoolyard. He would watch Helen play indoor baseball.

Notice that the reduced passage still sounds very much like Hemingway. Nothing has been changed that seems crucial to his style. Note too that although the revised passage is quite simple, none of the sentences is from the kernel. Hemingway is not innocent of transformations: he is relying on pronominalization, on a group of nominalizations, and, most notably, on a sequence of transformations responsible for what critics call the "*style indirect libre*." These transformations work this way:

[20] *The Short Stories of Ernest Hemingway* (New York, 1953), pp. 152–153.

(1) GT; quotation, or reported thought:

$$\text{He} \left\{\begin{array}{l}\text{thought}\\\text{said}\\\text{felt}\\\text{etc.}\end{array}\right\} \left. \begin{array}{l} \text{NP}_{\text{abst}} \\ \\ \\ \\ \text{She has made me lie}\end{array}\right\} \rightarrow \text{He thought, "She has made me lie"}$$

(2) Indirect discourse (change of pronouns and of verb tense):

He thought, "She has made me lie" → He thought that she had made him lie

(3) Deletion:

He thought that she had made him lie → She had made him lie[21]

The original passage, stripped of the effects of these transformations, reads as follows:

So his mother prayed for him and they stood up and Krebs kissed his mother and went out of the house. He thought this: I have tried so to keep my life from being complicated. Still, none of it has touched me. I have felt sorry for my mother and she has made me lie. I will go to Kansas City and get a job and she will feel all right about it. There will be one more scene maybe before I get away. I will not go down to my father's office. I will miss that one. I want my life to go smoothly. It has just gotten going that way. Well, that is all over now, anyway. I will go over to the schoolyard and watch Helen play indoor baseball.

[21] Morris Halle (Massachusetts Institute of Technology) explained these transformations to me. He is treating them in a forthcoming article on Virginia Woolf's style, and I make no attempt here to put the rules in proper and complete form. It should be noted though, that there is at present no justification for the grammar to contain rule number three as a transformation, since the transform is already generated by other rules.

The peculiar double vision of the style, the sense of the narrator peering into the character's mind and scrupulously reporting its contents, the possibility of distance and gentle irony—all these are gone with the transformational wind.

To be sure, these transformations do not in themselves distinguish Hemingway's style from the styles of many other writers (Virginia Woolf, Ford Madox Ford, James Joyce, etc.). But it is interesting, and promising, that a stylistic difference so huge as that between the Faulkner and Hemingway passages can be largely explained on the basis of so little grammatical apparatus.

Up to this point, I have been exploring some effects on style of particular transformations and groups of transformations, and arguing that this method of description has, potentially, considerable value for literary critics. But there are at least two other ways in which transformational machinery will aid the analyst of style.

First, it has often been pointed out that constructions may be left-branching ("Once George had left, the host and hostess gossiped briskly"), right-branching ("The host and hostess gossiped briskly, once George had left"), or self-embedding ("The host and hostess, once George had left, gossiped briskly"). Neither left- nor right-branching constructions tax the hearer's understanding, even when compounded at some length ("a very few not at all well liked union officials"; "the dog that worried the cat that chased the rat that ate the cheese that lay in the house that Jack built"). But layers of self-embedding quickly put too great a strain on the unaided memory ("the house in which the cheese that the rat that the cat that the dog worried chased ate lay was built by Jack"). Even a relatively small amount of self-embedding in a written passage can slow a reader down considerably.

With these preliminaries, consider the following sentence, which begins a short story:

She had practically, he believed, conveyed the intimation, the horrid, brutal, vulgar menace, in the course of their last dreadful conversation, when, for whatever was left him of pluck or confidence—confidence in what he would fain have called a little more aggressively the strength of his position—he had judged best not to take it up.[22]

The style is idiosyncratic in the highest degree, and the writer is, of course, Henry James. His special brand of complexity is impossible to unravel through the method I pursued with Faulkner. A number of *different* transformations are involved. But notice that most of this complexity results from self-embedding. With the embedded elements removed the sentence is still far from simple, but the Jamesian intricacy is gone:

She had practically conveyed the intimation in the course of their last dreadful conversation, when he had judged best not to take it up.

The following are the deleted sentences, with their full structure restored:

He believed [it].
[The intimation was a] horrid, brutal, vulgar menace.
[Something] was left him of pluck or confidence.
[It was] confidence in the strength of his position.
He would fain have called [it that], a little more aggressively.

[22] "The Bench of Desolation," *Ten Short Stories of Henry James,* ed. Michael Swan (London, 1948), p. 284.

The embedded elements, in short, significantly outweigh the main sentence itself, and needless to say, the strain on attention and memory required to follow the progress of the main sentence over and around so many obstacles is considerable. The difficulty, as well as the Jamesian flavor, is considerably lessened merely by substituting left- and right-branching constructions for self-embedding, even though all the kernel sentences are retained:

He believed that in the course of their last dreadful conversation she had practically conveyed the intimation, a horrid, brutal, vulgar menace, which he had then judged best not to take up, for whatever was left him of pluck or confidence— confidence in the strength of his position, as he would fain have called it, a little more aggressively.

It seems likely that much of James's later style can be laid to this syntactic device—a matter of *positioning* various constructions, rather than of favoring a few particular constructions. The relevance of positioning to style is, to be sure, no news. But again, transformational analysis should clarify the subject, both by providing descriptive rigor and by making available a set of alternatives to each complex sentence.

Finally, styles may also contrast in the kinds of transformational operations on which they are built. There are four possibilities: addition, deletion, reordering, and combination. Of these, my final sample depends heavily on deletion. The passage is from D. H. Lawrence's *Studies in Classic American Literature*, a book with an especially brusque, emphatic style, which results partly from Lawrence's affection for kernel sentences. But his main idiosyncrasy is the use of truncated sentences, which have gone through a variety of deletion transformations. Here is the excerpt:

The renegade hates life itself. He wants the death of life. So these many "reformers" and "idealists" who glorify the savages in America. They are death-birds, life-haters. Renegades.

We can't go back. And Melville couldn't. Much as he hated the civilized humanity he knew. He couldn't go back to the savages. He wanted to. He tried to. And he couldn't.

Because in the first place, it made him sick.[23]

With the deleted segments replaced, the passage reads, somewhat absurdly, like this:

The renegade hates life itself. He wants the death of life. So these many "reformers" and "idealists" who glorify the savages in America [want the death of life]. They are death-birds. [They are] life-haters. [They are] renegades.

We can't go back. And Melville couldn't [go back]. [Melville couldn't go back, as] much as he hated the civilized humanity he knew. He couldn't go back to the savages. He wanted to [go back to the savages]. He tried to [go back to the savages]. And he couldn't [go back to the savages].

[He couldn't go back to the savages] because, in the first place, it made him sick [to go back to the savages].

One does not need grammatical theory to see that Lawrence is deleting. But the restoration of the full form which is allowed by the grammar does reveal two interesting things. First, there is a large amount of repetition in the original passage, much more than actually shows. Perhaps this fact accounts for the driving insistence one feels in reading it. Second, Lawrentian deletion is a stylistic alternative to *conjunction*, which can also take place whenever there are two sentences partly alike in their constituents. The reasons for Lawrence's preferring deletion to conjunction might well be worth some study.

And in general, study of that sort should be the goal of

stylistic analysis. All I have done here is outline, briefly and in part informally, a fruitful method of stylistic *description*. But no *analysis* of a style, in the fuller sense, can get off the ground until there are adequate methods for the humble task of description. Such methods, I think, are provided by transformational grammar. Furthermore, I have argued, such a grammar is especially useful for this purpose in that it alone is powerful enough to set forth, formally and accurately, stylistic *alternatives* to a given passage or a given set of linguistic habits.

Now there is no reason to generalize from four passages to infinity, and in fact full stylistic descriptions of the work of even the four writers I have discussed would need to be far more elaborate than the sketches I have offered here. Moreover, many styles that readers perceive as distinctive are more complex in their syntactic patterns than these four. Finally, though syntax seems to be a central determinant of style, it is admittedly not the whole of style. Imagery, figures of speech, and the rest are often quite important. But to perform on various styles the kind of analysis I have attempted in this paper is to be convinced that transformational patterns constitute a significant part of what the sensitive reader perceives as style. Transformational analysis of literary discourse promises to the critic stylistic descriptions which are at once simpler and deeper than any hitherto available, and therefore more adequate foundations for critical interpretation. Not only that: if, as seems likely to happen, generative grammars with transformational rules help the linguist or critic to explicate convincingly the elusive but persistent notion of style, that achievement will stand as one more piece of evidence in favor of such grammars.

Metaphysical Criticism of Style

LOUIS T. MILIC

Louis T. Milic (1922-   ) was born in Yugoslavia but educated in America: his A. B., M. A., and Ph. D. degrees are
from Columbia University. He has taught English at Montana
State College and now teaches it at Columbia, where he is
director of college composition in the School of General
Studies. He has published articles on style in journals of
English; and his book, A Quantitative Approach to the Style
of Jonathan Swift, is in press. Like Steinmann's, Ohmann's,
and Sledd's essays, Milic's "Metaphysical Criticism of Style,"
an address delivered at the annual meeting of the Conference
on College Composition and Communication in 1966, finds
the concept of choice among synonymous expressions central
to stylistics ("Style must be defined in such a way that its
boundary with content can be clearly distinguished") and,
like Young and Becker's, Ohmann's, and Sledd's essays,
finds linguistics relevant to rhetoric. Intuitive, impressionistic,
metaphorical—in a word, metaphysical—descriptions of style
are, Milic believes, worthless; only quantitative descriptions
can be fruitful.

No wonder style interests so many—such interesting things have been said about it. Buffon, of course, is always mentioned: "Le style est l'homme même." Swift's famous aphorism is in the same category: "Proper words in proper places makes the true definition of a style." Alfred North Whitehead has told us that "style is the ultimate morality of mind." Who can resist Jean Cocteau's formulation, however oblique it may seem: "Style is not a dance: it is an overture"? And is there anyone who does not feel better informed when he learns what Hemingway has said about his own style: "In stating as fully as I could how things really were, it was often very difficult and I wrote awkwardly and the awkwardness is that they called my style."[1]

These statements are among the best-known or the best-formulated of the hundreds of axioms, aphorisms and apothegms on style, but they are fully typical in two respects. They all seem to mean something, something that we ought to find instructive. And they strive by wit, paradox and imagery, to express the ineffable. The struggle with the reluctant medium of words is concealed, though it can be sensed in the high density of such statements. But when we examine the propositional content of these sayings and find it tautological, obvious, contradictory or simply absent, we realize that

[1] Buffon, "Discours sur le style," *Oeuvres Philosophiques,* ed. Jean Piveteau (Paris, 1954), p. 500; Swift, "A Letter to a Young Gentleman," *Irish Tracts and Sermons,* ed. Herbert Davis (Oxford, 1948), p. 65; Whitehead, *The Organisation of Thought* (London, 1917), p. 25; Cocteau, *Oeuvres Completes* (Geneva, 1950), X, 355 ["Le style n'est pas une danse, c'est une demarche,"]; A. E. Hotchner, "Hemingway Talks to American Youth," *This Week,* Oct. 18, 1959, p. 11.

Address delivered at the Conference on College Composition and Communication, March 25, 1966, Denver, Colorado. With revisions, April, 1966. Reprinted by permission of the author.

they do not really contribute to our understanding of the problem of style, however much they may enlighten us about the feelings of those who said them. For words, if they are arranged in a certain way (even by a random sentence-generator), have a constant tendency to mean, in Professor Wimsatt's phrase. But this kind of haphazard meaning is incomplete and leads to the metaphysical.[2]

Everyone who has tried to say something about an author's style has probably committed this kind of fault. He has read, let us say, a very impressive writer, and he is full of the desire to say what possessed him and what fascinated him about the writer's language, but he has nothing to fall back on except burning intensity and the tendency of sentences to mean something. Professor Trilling has truly said: "It is notoriously difficult to dispute about style in a coherent and rational way. But it is not difficult to dispute about style in *some* way."[3]

The reader of these disputes must make allowances, for he has no means of judging the criticism of style. In this department of literary study, there seems to be no generally accepted method. Though biography is not a science, some canons of historical description obtain there, and biographical writing is judged by those standards. Bibliography has stated requirements and textual criticism is even more particular. It should be noted that no aphorisms are extant of the type "Bibliography is the

[2] The term *metaphysical* is used in two ways in this paper: loosely, to describe any criticism of style that is not usefully quantitative; and strictly, to describe any statement not verifiable even in principle. The details of my classification are set out schematically in the outline provided in the Appendix.

[3] Lionel Trilling, "The Two Environments: Reflections on the Study of English," *Encounter*, XXV (1965), 9.

order of the cosmos" or "Textual criticism is not a grave minuet, but a marathon upon all fours."

Stylistics, however, has for most scholars still no method beyond the method of impressionistic description and a vague use of rhetoric. But even those who describe the style of a writer in terms of the impression they have received scarcely seem to be aware of the nature of such descriptions. A description of style, when it is not quantitative, can only be figurative. Such a description tends to rely on comparisons, analogies and similarly crude approximations. Of course, even impressionistic descriptions can be responsible and verifiable, e.g., "Swift depends on seriation" or "Johnson is given to antithetic parallel clauses." But few impressionistic critics are satisfied with such tame accounts of their responses. They have their eyes on the empyrean.

I became most keenly aware of this when I was studying the style of Jonathan Swift.[4] Nearly all critics have praised it and some have tried to describe it. When all these descriptions are placed side by side, they amount to little more than a glossary of adjectives: *charming, clear, common, concise, correct, direct, elaborate, elegant, energetic, graceful, hard-round-crystalline, homely, lucid, manly, masculine, muscular, nervous, ornamented, perfect, plain, poor, proper, pure, salty, simple, sinewy, sonorous, vigorous.* This is far from a complete list, but it suggests some of the shortcomings of this method of description.

Though *clear* may seem to refer specifically to the writing process, it actually describes the response of the reader. What is clear to one may not be to another.

[4] See my forthcoming, *A Quantitative Approach to the Style of Jonathan Swift* (The Hague, in press).

Similarly, with *lucid, simple, plain*; the attention is on the reader, not on the writing. *Simple* describes nothing in the writing, unless it is specified as referring to particular predicates of simplicity, such as sentence structure, choice of word, modification, sentence order, for example. Absolutes like *pure* and *perfect* describe nothing at all, but are merely assertions by the critic that the writer is without flaw. Such terms as *muscular, nervous, sinewy*, drawing as they do from various parts of the writer's anatomy, reveal the critic's desire to move from the style to the man, or to use the man to describe the style.

The difficulties of description are clearly great enough to drive a man to desperation. For example, F. L. Lucas in the space of two pages describes Swift as "a lean gray wolf, with white fangs bared" and says he is like a Pennine moorland not like the Highlands.[5] Somerset Maugham presses the landscape analogy even harder, calling Swift's style a placid French canal whereas Dryden's is a cheerful English river.[6]

Any critic is capable of a far-fetched or outrageous metaphor on occasion, but descriptions of style pullulate with this kind of thing. In part this is the result of a certain confusion of terms, which reflects a theoretical disorganization in this field of criticism. The very meaning of the term *style* is in question. In common speech, style is always *somehow, somewhat* or *in a manner* whatever it is: "His style was somehow reminiscent of a tight steel spring." Or it is joined to another term roughly synonymous: *his style and manner, his style and outlook,*

---

[5] *Style* (London, 1955), pp. 210, 126.
[6] *The Summing-Up* (New York, 1957), pp. 20–21.

his style and tone. And the term is always modified, usually by adjectives: *a lapidary, an elegant, a personal, a drab, a breathless, a mannered* or *an affected style.*

Implicit in all these usages is a nebulous sense that style is what distinguishes individuals from one another, especially in their linguistic behavior. But the efficacy of the technical term has been compromised by its use as a word of all work, expressing a mere *je-ne-sais-quoi* of distinctiveness. This slipshod kind of definition leads to metaphysical stylistics, which does nothing to advance understanding and a good deal to retard progress in the method and the practice of criticism.

To be studied effectively, style must be defined in such a way that its boundary with content can be clearly distinguished. Whether it is considered the sum of a writer's deviations from the linguistic norm or his characteristic features of expression is not material. Both imply the same requirements for effective study: a knowledge of the background against which he is trying to stand out and a means of stating his degree of distinctiveness. A feature of style, whether it be a favored area of the vocabulary, a preference in imagery, a rhetorical habit or tendency to have recourse to certain syntactical patterns, must be described in concrete and verifiable terms, which finally means, in quantitative terms.

It is precisely this understandable reluctance to deal in quantities, in *parameters* of style, which has forced reputable scholars into gross errors and primitive distortions. Any statistician will point out that sampling is crucial in statistical demonstration. In dealing with a large corpus of any kind, if we cannot examine all of it, we must content ourselves with a sample. Most scholars proceed as if all samples, regardless how drawn, were equivalent in quality, which is the same as saying that any part is typical of the whole and that any part typifies every part. This is plainly not so, yet it is implicit in much scholarly work concerned with style.

An interesting example is found in the question of Henry James's later prose. Around 1905, when he began to prepare the New York edition of his works, he extensively revised the language of his novels. His early novel *Roderick Hudson* was first published in 1876 and in a revised version a few years later. When it emerged from the final revision, it was considerably changed. In 1924, Helene Harvitt asserted, in a published paper, that James's revisions had disfigured his work, making it "labored, heavy, ambiguous and sometimes almost impenetrable."[7] She illustrated this thesis with examples drawn from the versions of *Roderick Hudson*.[8] In his book on Henry James, F. O. Matthiessen undertook to refute this charge, claiming that James's revisions had generally resulted in improvements. But he conducted his refutation by examining the revisions of a different book, *The Portrait of a Lady*.[9]

The suggestion that the study of style must be pursued by rigorous means derived from linguistics and the quantitative sciences is likely to find no favor among literary scholars. Nonetheless, it seems to be the inevitable direction such work must take. Intuitive impressionism cannot often lead to productive results. I shall

[7] "How Henry James Revised *Roderick Hudson*: A Study in Style," *PMLA*, XXIX (1924), 203–227.

[8] Raymond D. Havens has noted that Helene Harvitt's "first" edition was really the thoroughly-revised second ("The Revision of *Roderick Hudson*," *PMLA*, XL [1925], 433).

[9] Appendix: "The Painter's Sponge and Varnish Bottle," in *Henry James: The Major Phase* (New York, 1963), pp. 152–186.

not illustrate this contention by citing the naive attempts to attribute works to an author by internal evidence, which consist mainly of claiming that some lexical items are present in large numbers (unstated) and that no one but X could therefore have written Y.

No, the kind of thing I have in mind is exemplified by the following comment:

When we call Newman's prose concrete and particular, we do not, I think, mean to suggest that it is . . . particularly attentive to the minute surface details of experience. . . . an examination of the *Apologia* suggests that the particular and concrete rarely appear except as internal impression transmuted from thing into idea or feeling. And this leads to the problem of how Newman's style appears to create a living felt reality while at the same time it remains largely abstract, one might almost say eighteenth-century, not only in its rhythms and diction but in the generalizing force of its language.[10]

The writer casts his impression—that Newman's prose is concrete—in the teeth of the fact that he knows it is abstract. His struggle consists of trying to find a way to join these opposites by violence together. This is truly metaphysical, both in Johnson's sense of the term and in the common sense, as belonging to a different order of reality, one in which the ordinary rules of evidence do not apply.

That this kind of defective criticism is not merely a chance aberration but a regular aspect of reputable scholarship can be amply documented. Here for instance is a comment on the style of C. P. Snow, part of a critical biography:

[10] George Levine, "The Prose of the *Apologia Pro Vita Sua*," *Victorian Newsletter*, No. 27 (Spring 1965), p. 5.

Snow's prose, as well, is marked by plainness, an innocuous prose that rarely does more than indicate essentials. His style is, as it were, virtually an absence of style when we use the word to signify something distinctive. There is, also, a curious lack of development in his power of expression from first novel to last, as though Snow refused to tamper with something that he considered adequate.[11]

A bit further on, the writer says that the prose calls for parody and that Snow uses the word *diffident* in the same way in passages written twenty years apart. The first sentence of the quotation says the prose is plain, an assertion verifiable only in principle, for we have no sure criteria of plainness. The claim that Snow has no style is a hackneyed paradox belied by the writer's own evidence, for parody can deal only with the distinctive and a favorite word is of course a distinctive feature. The claim that Snow's style lacks development reveals merely that Snow's critic does not admire Snow's style.

My third example has a peculiar interest because of the height to which it builds on sand:

Wordsworth's prose is admirable. It is seldom magnificent. 'It does not sparkle,' said Nowell C. Smith justly. As a prose stylist, Wordsworth lacks the clarity of Dryden, the force of Hazlitt, the passion of Milton, the metaphorical daring of Coleridge, the simultaneous levels of either Swift or Lamb, and the opulence of an admirer who borrowed power from Wordsworth, De Quincey. And yet Wordsworth practiced to a viable degree clarity, force, passion, strength of metaphor, levels at least of scorn, and richness if not opulence. He achieved what he most wanted, the signature of personal conviction.[12]

[11] Frederick R. Karl, *C. P. Snow: The Politics of Conscience* (Carbondale, Ill., 1963), p. 9.

[12] Carl R. Woodring, *Wordsworth* (Boston, 1965), p. 133.

The first two sentences alone would not puzzle anyone: Wordsworth's prose is worthy to be admired, though it lacks the quality of magnificence (or sparkle). But when the passage goes on with its list of abstractions assigned to other writers, it surely requires us to know what these abstractions stand for, which is questionable. Anyway, how is *force* to be told from *passion, richness* from *opulence?* And are "levels of scorn" an aspect of style? When, finally, the writer says that Wordsworth had in some vague degree these vague qualities, he has not greatly added to our knowledge. His conclusion, to the extent that we can decipher it, is either metaphysical or not about style at all.

Though it would be valuable to be able to infer the mental processes of an author from his style, no means exist for doing so. A claim of that sort often passes unnoticed, possibly because statements about style are not taken very seriously anyway, but it would be good to know how such a conclusion as this one could be validated:

For all its quietness, however, the prose of *Dombey and Son* is consistently hard, compact and unsparing. Its economy comes from the fact that Dickens knew at each moment just what he wanted to say and said it without hesitation.[13]

Passing over the adjectives as mere decoration, we can wonder how the critic knew what he asserts to be a fact about Dickens, even granting that the "economy" of the style could be derived from it.

Another type of questionable assertion is made in this discussion of the style of Ruskin:

[13] Steven Marcus, *Dickens: From Pickwick to Dombey* (New York, 1965), p. 293.

Ruskin had a painful story to tell and evolved a style which enabled the telling to be both ingratiating and true. The writing is remarkably colloquial, yet taut with ironies which he directs at his parents or himself. What appears to be an ingenuous ecstasy of pure presentation was the product of a lifelong effort to suppress all evidence of laboriousness, to substitute the suppleness of speech for the formalities of rhetoric. Through a triumph of style, Ruskin made his most sophisticated prose on his most complex subject read as if it were mere artless causerie.[14]

If we take "mere artless causerie" to be a synonym for "colloquial writing," we are faced with an incredible paradox, achieved through a "triumph of style." Ruskin perhaps labored to make his prose informal. The exaggerated assertion that he succeeded must be laid to the critic's inability wholly to believe this and therefore to convey it demonstratively. Such a statement about Ruskin requires some demonstration.

Writers about style usually do not trouble to demonstrate anything, except by single instances. Consider the difficulties of demonstrating the assertion in the following encomium of Henry James:

On the whole, for richness, for subtlety, for attention to concords of sense and sound, James's later style was the most remarkable style in English since the 17th century. With all its artifices, there is something elemental about it. Unlike the virtuoso styles, admirable though they are, of a Stevenson or a Swinburne, that of James refers us back, not to the eloquence of the author, but to the resources of the language.[15]

[14] John D. Rosenberg, *The Darkening Glass* (New York, 1961), pp. 218–219.

[15] F. W. Dupee, *Henry James* (New York, 1951), pp. 195–196.

Though we may differ about the meaning of *remarkable*, we can agree that over 250 years have elapsed since the 17th century. We are surely not asked to believe that the critic has examined all the remarkable styles in those centuries and has declared James the winner. No, like most such claims it is hyperbole and does not refer to anything, any more than *elemental* does or the reference to Stevenson and Swinburne or the resources of the language. It is all metaphysics, demonstrable in principle, but not on earth, and is just a form of praise disguised as a description.

My last exhibit is from Lionel Trilling:

As for the style of the book, it is not less than definitive in American literature. The prose of *Huckleberry Finn* established for written prose the virtues of American colloquial speech. This has nothing to do with pronunciation or grammar. It has something to do with the structure of the sentence, which is simple, direct, and fluent, maintaining the rhythm of the word-groups of speech and the intonations of the speaking voice.

Out of his knowledge of the actual speech of America Mark Twain forged a classic prose. The adjective may seem a strange one, yet it is apt. Forget the misspellings and the faults of grammar, and the prose will be seen to move with the greatest simplicity, directness, lucidity and grace.[16]

The prose of *Huckleberry Finn* is colloquial. But why this eminent critic should wish to say that Mark Twain accomplished this effect without grammar is not easy to understand. Take out the grammar and the misspellings and do you have the same prose, the same Huck Finn?

[16] "Huckleberry Finn," in *The Liberal Imagination* (New York, 1950), pp. 115–116, 117.

This curious reluctance to be specific and concrete, to admit that style is first of all made up of certain kinds of linguistic units betrays a distrust of available methods of discussing style.

It is all rather dispiriting; from Morris Croll to Spitzer, Ullmann, Josephine Miles and Herdan, there is a bulky literature of stylistics, with something for every taste. And yet the great majority of scholars are without any knowledge of it. They write about style in a Rhetoric of Metaphysics, whose main components are remoteness from the facts of language, a reluctance to believe that style can be concretely described and romantic exaggeration.

It is my impression that some of this disorder may derive from the debilitating belief that style and content are inseparable and the resulting unwillingness to attempt anything that might seem to show trust in their disjunction. The organic theory of Croce seems to have given special impetus to metaphysical discussion of style because of Croce's explicit distrust of anything smacking of the technical, especially rhetoric. Yet this ancient discipline, whatever its deficiencies in an age that has abandoned formal studies, did furnish a method for both the study of literature and the teaching of composition.

The perpetuation of this corrupt tradition of commentary about style is productive of a number of evil effects. In the study of literature, where the habit of precise and responsible thinking is highly desirable, it encourages habits of slipshod and haphazard thinking which undermine the whole process. Large and vague generalizations, conclusions without evidence, atypical examples, paradoxes and contradictions, words used without understanding and sheer nonsense embellish the pages of our students' critical essays. These defects are surely related to the criticism I have described.

An even more immediate consequence of this same criticism is manifested in the teaching of composition. Here, especially in the correction of essays, stylistic criticism is the foremost means of instruction. If it has no sounder basis than metaphysics, how can the student learn? To improve, he must know what his mistakes are and how to correct them. These tasks require commentary with a high degree of specificity. The summarizing comment which lurks malevolently at the end of a student's paper usually announces its consanguinity to the literary examples I cited earlier. This quotation from a well-known textbook betrays its metaphysical ancestry: "This is the style you've been working for: not too big, not too little, sensible, clear, on its toes. You are touching the concrete beautifully."[17] The student may gather that he has done something right, but how can he discover what it was, unless it be concerned with gymnastics?

What is to be done? A great deal of skepticism about such euphonious vacuities as I have quoted is evidently necessary. Metaphysical stylistics is a rewarding study for the skeptic, and the evidence of its defects can be gathered by anyone who can read, count and reason. It is also obvious that sane and useful criticism of style can no longer proceed without some technical knowledge of the language and of rhetoric or without reference to available systems of stylistic analysis.

Unlike the critics I have cited, Aristotle did not allow his Metaphysics to contaminate his Poetics. In fact, his

---

[17] Sheridan Baker, *The Practical Stylist* (New York, 1962), p. 133.

Poetics contains three technical chapters (on parts of speech, figurative words, and word-choice) which we are always being urged to ignore. We should be foolish to do so, for analysis cannot proceed without technical detail or it becomes metaphysical by default.

APPENDIX

A RHETORIC OF METAPHYSICAL STYLISTICS
Outline of a Classification

I Statements *not* really about style
II Statements about style
   A Pure Metaphysical (referring to a different order of reality)
   B Verifiable
     1 Only in principle
     2 In practice
       a Erroneous in fact
       b Correct
         (1) Useless
           (a) Obvious
           (b) Tautological
         (2) Useful
           (a) Possibly: Impressionistic
           (b) Generally: Quantitative*

* Not metaphysical; therefore does not properly belong in this classification.

Coordination (Faulty) and Subordination (Upside-Down)

JAMES SLEDD

James Sledd (1914-   ) was born in Georgia and educated at Emory and Oxford Universities and the University of Texas. At Oxford, he was a Rhodes scholar. He has taught at Duke and Northwestern Universities and the Universities of Chicago, California (Berkeley), and Texas, where he is now professor of English. Among his works are *Dr. Johnson's Dictionary* (1955), with Gwin J. Kolb; *A Short Introduction to English Grammar* (1959), which has an excellent chapter on English prose style; and *Dictionaries and THAT Dictionary* (1962), with Wilma R. Ebbitt. "Coordination (Faulty) and Subordination (Upside-Down)," an address delivered at the annual meeting of the Conference on College Composition and Communication in 1956, is a contribution of structural linguistics to stylistics. The traditional rhetorical doctrine about the use of coordination and subordination rests, Sledd believes, upon an assumption that structural linguistics has shown to be false: "that grammatical and semantic categories . . . coincide," a variant of another false assumption, that "form and meaning are inseparable." Consequently, the concept of choice among synonymous expressions is, for Sledd, as for Steinmann, Ohmann, and Milic, indispensable.

(This paper attributes certain opinions to "the linguist," a fictitious individual whose authority I find it convenient to cite for opinions of my own, and certain others to "the traditionalist," a hollow man who is never allowed to talk back. For these innocent inventions, perhaps no actual linguist living or dead would care to be responsible.)

The first and most important way in which linguistics can serve us as teachers of composition is that it can help us see what we have to do and how we can best do it. The teacher who knows some linguistics sees the composition course in the light of his knowledge; and if he does not foolishly conclude that linguistics is a panacea, his introduction to linguistic science may be part of a general reorientation which is more valuable than any one specific use of linguistic methods or materials. Linguistics can teach us something about the relations between speech and writing—for example, that speech comes first in time and in importance, that writing is an incomplete but partially independent secondary representation of speech, that the kinds of speech which we normally write are very different from plain talk, and that mastering these differences is a large part of our students' job. Linguistics can teach us something about the nature of style as choice; and when we are dealing with style in language, it can give us the necessary terms and distinctions to describe the choices that are open. Linguistics can teach us that grammatical structure is stylistically no less important than vocabulary and that structure must be described systematically, *as* a system

From *College Composition and Communication,* VII (December, 1956), 181–187. Reprinted with the permission of the National Council of Teachers of English and the author.

and as a *formal* system, whose categories cannot be adequately defined in terms of meaning. And linguistics has already taught us that when we have specified the choices which the student can make in speech and writing, we should not ruin our work by upholding some silly standard of mechanical correctness. A good linguist is no *enemy* of standards, but he does believe that we should know what is before we try to say what ought to be. He can therefore help us, I think, to set higher ideals than we have often been contented with—and to reach them, too.

If this faith that is in me is more than the faith of an apprentice witch-doctor in a new and blacker magic, I must welcome the demand that the linguist and his converts put up or shut up. I do welcome it, and happily accept my share in the burden of proof that the principles of linguistics are directly relevant to problems of writing. Such proof, in one small area, is what I am here to offer.

A grammatical system, the linguist says, is a formal structure whose categories must be formally defined. His reason is not only that it is difficult to deal precisely and objectively with meaning. Grammatical and logical categories, he argues, do not always coincide; even if they did, the logical or semantic categories which would have to be recognized in the description of a particular language would still be determined by the number and nature of the formal distinctions in that language; and if grammar is to be a means of interpretation, the grammarian must start with the forms in order to avoid circularity. It is only by way of the forms that we can get at the meanings.

These propositions, if they are true, have the most

immediate and far-reaching consequences for the teaching of composition. Both our descriptions and our prescriptions will have to be revised. With at least some of the necessary changes in description all of us are familiar. The conservative himself is now a little uneasy when he tells a class that a noun is the name of a person, place, or thing, that the subject of a sentence is what the sentence is about, or that a sentence itself is a group of words that expresses a complete thought. The junior witch-doctor, like me, is more than just uneasy. He begins his definition of the English noun by describing its inflections; he goes on to note the main positions which nouns occupy in phrases and sentences; he says something about the derivational patterns in which nouns occur; and he strictly subordinates his semantic descriptions to these matters of form. Happily or unhappily, witch-hunters and witch-doctors both recognize that in description a revolution has begun.

Perhaps we have not yet recognized so clearly that the changes in grammatical description which have been forced upon us will force us also to change our statements of what is good and what is bad in our students' speech and writing. Ultimately, we cannot escape that recognition. If we accept the linguist's doctrines, we will find that our whole treatment of diction must be modified, and modified at every level of our teaching, from the freshman classroom to the graduate seminar. A good example is our classification of clauses and our instructions for the use of coordination and subordination.

Our usual teaching about clauses rests, I think, on the false assumption that grammatical and semantic categories do coincide. Having made that assumption, we quite logically tell our students to put their main ideas into main clauses and their subordinate ideas into subordinate clauses. Principal clauses, we tell them, express principal ideas, so that compound sentences, consisting of two or more such clauses, give equal emphasis to equal thoughts but weaken unity or coherence. Between the clauses of a compound sentence, which we say are related just as separate sentences are related, there is then no logical advance; two ideas, or two expressions of the same idea (if two are possible), are merely juxtaposed. With complex sentences, we say, the case is altered. Since subordinate clauses express subordinate ideas, complex sentences rank and relate our thoughts in the order of their importance. The primary thought receives primary emphasis, and complex sentences are therefore more unified and more coherent than compound sentences.

I have been careful not to misrepresent the traditional theory of clauses, which I have found in learned histories of prose style as well as a variety of handbooks; and I think I am equally fair in saying that to a linguist, this theory seems to rest on a series of bad puns, the old confusion of grammatical and logical terms. Subordinate clauses, the linguist tells us, are grammatically subordinate; that is, they are used like single nouns, adjectives, or adverbs, often to expand smaller constructions. Just as we can say, for example, "The man is my uncle," so we can expand the nominal construction *the man* with a subordinate clause and say, "The man *whom you met* is my uncle." In this grammatical sense, *whom you met* is subordinate, precisely as we might say that *big* is subordinate in the sentence, "The big man is my nephew," or that *there* is subordinate in "The boy there is my nephew." Similarly, according to the linguist, independent or principal clauses are *grammatically* independent; they are subject-predicate combinations which do not expand smaller constructions and whose only *grammatical* equivalents are similar combinations. It does *not* follow that the same state of affairs *must* always be symbolized or *should* always be symbolized by the same clause-pattern. Principal clauses can and sometimes should express subordinate ideas, which need not be expressed by grammatical subordination; and the clauses of a compound sentence may be as unified and coherent and as precisely related as the clauses of a *complex* sentence. The traditional theory of clauses is simply untenable. When we teach it, we are teaching a rhetoric that is bad because we have confused our grammar with our logic.

The most obviously false statement in the traditional theory is the least generally accepted, that compound sentences, by comparison with complex sentences, lack unity, coherence, and precise articulation. I will not laboriously disprove this statement, either by analyzing the meanings of words like *and* or *but* or by citing the logician's rules for the transformation of propositions from one form to another; our everyday experience is ample refutation of an obvious absurdity.

Other propositions in the traditional theory turn out to be less clear, but more dangerous, because more plausible and more widely believed. One version might be summed up in the ambiguous platitude that form and meaning are inseparable. Thus when he lays down his rules about clauses, the traditionalist may mean that in their use we have no stylistic choice, because it is impossible to say the same thing in two different clause-patterns; "the writer's meaning *is* his language, and his language *is* his meaning."[1] We should therefore tell our students, when their use of subordination or coordination displeases us, only that they should re-think their material and say what they really mean.

If this is what the traditionalist intends, his theory is easily reduced to absurdity, for it denies the possibility of translation, paraphrase, summary, accurate indirect quotation, and deductive logic. Indeed, if there were no synonymous expressions, language and communication themselves would be impossible, since meanings would be inseparably bound to particular sequences of phones or graphs. If we asked a man what he meant, he could only repeat what he had said before, and if we did not understand him, he could give no further explanation.

The second step in the refutation of this wild notion is again the appeal to the logician's transformation-rules, which guarantee the possibility of expressing the same content in clauses of different form. So if we say, "Either it's not raining, or the streets are wet," we have uttered a compound sentence; but that compound sentence may be exactly translated by the *complex* sentence, "If it's raining, the streets are wet." Such transformations are the stock in trade of the logician, who puts his propositions into the form that best suits his purpose; and we do precisely the same thing unless we have lost our senses by reading the New Critics. Consider the following pairs of sentences:

1. Though he was tired, he still worked hard.

   He was tired, but he still worked hard.

2. Language would be impossible, since meanings

[1] This quotation is genuine, but no good purpose would be served by identifying its authors, who must have written it in their sleep.

would be inseparably bound to particular phones.
Language would be impossible, for meanings would
be inseparably bound to particular phones.

3. I won't write you, since I wouldn't have anything
to say.

²I won't ³write you² | ²I wouldn't have anything to
³say¹#

The members of each pair, though one sentence is complex and the other compound, are the same in meaning.

To my examples it may be objected that although two
sentences may say the same thing, they say it with different emphases—that main clauses are by nature more
emphatic than subordinate clauses. Such an objection
would embody the traditional theory in its most limited
but clearest, most persuasive, and most generally accepted form. For all that, I answer that the objection is
preposterous; and the form of my answer proves that the
answer is correct. The sentence "I answer that the objection is preposterous" does not emphasize the mere fact
that I am meeting an objection, though that fact is stated
in the main clause. Rather the emphasis is on the subordinate clause, "that the objection is preposterous," and
as far as I can tell the sentence would not be improved
by reversing this arrangement.

Better examples than my own are of course a dime a
dozen. Turning the pages of Kruisinga's big grammar,[2]
I quickly find numbers of good sentences in which a
nominal clause is more emphatic than the main clause
that it depends on:

It was generally discovered that the maker of these splendid
books was himself a splendid old man.

[2] E. Kruisinga, *A Handbook of Present-Day English*, Part II, Vol. 3
(5th ed., Groningen, 1932), pp. 367, 373, 375, 376, 379, 381, etc.

The fact was that Yeobright's fame had spread to an awkward extent before he left home.

A good deal of its importance consists in this, that it is minute and detailed.

As for adjectival clauses, Kruisinga actually sets up a special class among them, defined as giving additional information "which is not subordinate to the rest of the sentence but of equal weight." From his discussion, one can gather many convincing specimens:

She was much attracted by the novels of Kingsley, between whose genius and his faults she drew a drastic contrast.

Eustacia was indoors in the dining-room, which was really more like a kitchen, having a stone floor and a gaping chimney-corner.

It is a point that we must exert our imaginations a little to understand.

To complete the roll call of clause-types, I will here just mention certain kinds of sentence where the main idea almost has to go in an adverbial clause in order to avoid absurdity:

As the years passed, I grew wiser.

When Lincoln was assassinated, my father was a young man.

Before the war began, Joe went to America.

In most contexts it would be plain silly to write, "As I grew wiser, the years passed"; yet the passage of time is certainly more important than any individual's increase in wisdom. The traditionalist will have to say, when he is faced with these sentences, that coordination and sub-ordination need not reflect the intrinsic importance of ideas, but only their importance to the writer.

The evasion will not save him from the ultimate necessity of junking his theory, deliberately writing bad sentences, or deliberately wrecking good ones: the most telling of all the instances in which the traditional theory fails to account for the facts are those where it would require damaging revision. Consistency would require the traditionalist, for example, to revise the following neat sentence from Kruisinga's collection:

The noise echoed terribly through the building, and then there was a silence that was even more terrible.

To my mind, that sentence emphasizes the fact that the silence was more terrible than the noise, and I assume that the professional who wrote it knew and wrote what he intended; but the traditionalist must spoil the sentence because he cannot leave the main idea in a subordinate clause. He will have to write something awful, like this:

The noise echoed terribly through the building, and then the silence was even more terrible.

In the same way, he will have to ruin my next example, where again an empty main clause actually contributes to emphasis:

It is not everybody that cares for early Staffordshire pottery.

The edge would be quite taken off of that admirable generalization if it were revised:

Not everybody cares for early Staffordshire pottery.

And so it goes, in sentence after sentence. The traditionalist, however, is determined to uphold standards even though he has none worth upholding. It is thus that he promotes vice in the name of virtue.

I suggest, then, in summarizing the critical part of this paper, that the linguist's general insistence on the formal nature of grammatical categories will force us to delete specific sections from our handbooks—namely all instructions to put main ideas in main clauses and subordinate ideas in subordinate clauses. "Determine the most important idea of the sentence," the typical handbook says, "and express it in the main clause. Put lesser ideas in subordinate clauses, phrases, or words."[3] I think I have shown that that rule will do more harm than good; and if I am right, the demonstration has positive value and cannot be dismissed as merely negative. I am still not content with the mere deletion of a bad rule. We will have to put something in its place if we are to teach the student anything about the use of principal and subordinate clauses; and I should like to offer some modest suggestions, centering on the analysis of a few sentences such as we typically use for horrible examples.

If grammatical and logical terms cannot be equated and if we can say the same thing in different clause-patterns, then the student must regularly face stylistic choices which cannot be made mechanically. He must learn that writing is purposeful, that good writing is writing that serves its purpose well, and that the real abnegation of standards is the assumption that a single kind of writing is the only correct kind for all purposes. He may then grasp the possibility of reasoned choice by various criteria, one of which, in the matter of clauses, is proper emphasis. An idea may be emphasized by making a separate sentence of the clause which expresses it, by giving that clause a certain position within a larger sentence, by balancing or contrasting its structure with

[3] This quotation is also genuine, but too familiar to need identification.

that of other clauses, or in some cases (as my examples have shown) by subordinating the important clause. Sometimes different clause-patterns will be equally emphatic, and the choice of *for* or *since, though* or *but, who* or *and he* will have to be made by some other standard—variety, rhythm, ease in transition, or the like.

Since stylistic choices are so complicated, and since we cannot trust the traditional rules to decide them, we will have to replace the old rules of thumb with a more detailed analysis, both formal and semantic, of the patterns of clause-connection and sentence-connection in English; and we must try to invent exercises which will turn the student's theoretical knowledge into active control of the resources of his language. For example, *but* and *though* may be synonymous; often they both indicate that the simultaneous truth of the two propositions which they connect is for some reason not to be expected or out of the ordinary. The differences between *but* and *though* are largely formal: *though*-clauses are grammatically subordinate and rather freely moveable, while *but*-clauses are grammatically independent and must follow a *preceding* independent clause. These facts could easily be impressed on the student's mind by asking him to observe the effects of replacing *but* by *though* in a collection of sentences or throughout a single long passage.

I would add, however, that a great deal of our trouble with subordination and coordination is not grammatical at all, but logical or rhetorical; and here I come to my analysis of horrible examples. In the following sentence, all of us would object to the faulty coordination:

The barometer's falling, and those clouds have wind in them, and we'd better put into harbor at once.

Certainly the sentence is bad, but not because it contains three independent clauses; we would not object to sentences like the following:

He laughed, and he laughed, and he laughed.

Fox singled, and Minoso doubled, and the game was won.

In that one morning it rained, and it hailed, and it snowed.

Since the difference between the accepted and rejected sentences is not in their clause-patterns, which are identical, we must look for it elsewhere; and it is easy to see that by the label "faulty coordination" we actually mean, in this instance, a failure in logic. In the sentence about the barometer, the suggested relation of premise and conclusion, situation and consequence, is not made clear; and any rewriting will be acceptable if it introduces the needed clarity. A first rewriting changes the one sentence into two and makes their relation clear by inference from their relative positions:

The barometer's falling, and those clouds have wind in them. We'd better put into harbor at once.

Two other rewritings make the relation explicit, but in notably different patterns of coordination and subordination:

We'd better put into harbor at once; for the barometer's falling, and those clouds have wind in them.

Since the barometer's falling and those clouds have wind in them, we'd better put into harbor at once.

Unless the original sentence were placed in a determining context, there would be little to choose, for all their differences in clause-patterns, among the three corrections.

Of my next example, the usual criticism would be "upside-down subordination":

He had almost reached Gainesville when he saw the tornado that struck the town and killed two hundred people.

One man's arrival in town, most of us would say, is not so important as the death of two hundred people—which is no doubt true, but irrelevant to the judgment of the sentence. The sentence is bad because its first two clauses state that two things happened about the same time, while the third clause has nothing to do with this temporal relation; and the fault will remain if the unimportant first clause is subordinated and the important third clause is made independent and coordinate with the second:

When he had almost reached Gainesville, he saw the tornado, and it struck the town and killed two hundred people.

As a matter of fact, it is almost indifferent which of the first two clauses is introduced by *when*, but in either case the third clause must be made a separate sentence:

When he had almost reached Gainesville, he saw the tornado. It struck the town and killed two hundred people.

He had almost reached Gainesville when he saw the tornado. It struck the town and killed two hundred people.

The really applicable rule would not be to avoid upside-down subordination, but to talk about one thing at a time.

I would conclude, from my two horrible examples, that when we have given a student a theoretical and practical knowledge of English clause-patterns, the best general advice that we can next give him is to use both coordination and subordination in such a way that the natural or logical relations in his material will be clear. When he puts one sentence after another, when he puts two clauses together in a single sentence, or when he chooses a conjunction or a pair of intonation-patterns to connect his clauses, he is building, at the same time, a pattern of meanings. Neither we nor the linguist can decide for the student what he wants that pattern to be; but we *can* show him any formal indications of contradiction or confusion in his finished product. We can insist that he talk sense; and though when we do so we have quite properly left the realm of grammar for those of logic and rhetoric, our insistence will be more effective if our grammar has been sensible—that is, if we have abandoned, among other delusions, the identification of main and subordinate ideas with main and subordinate clauses.

Style and Good Style

MONROE C. BEARDSLEY

Monroe C. Beardsley (1915-   ) was born in Connecticut and educated at Yale University. He has taught at Yale, Mount Holyoke, and Swarthmore, where he is now professor of philosophy. Among his works are *Practical Logic* (1950) and *Aesthetics: Problems in the Philosophy of Criticism* (1958). Beardsley is a philosopher; but his interest in aesthetics has led him to rhetoric, in particular to stylistics. His "Style and Good Style," an address delivered at a National Defense Education Act Institute for Advanced Study in English in 1965, is (among other things) an able, spirited defense of a view that Steinmann, Ohmann, Milic, and Sledd attack: namely, that form and meaning are inseparable. Consequently, far from finding the concept of choice among synonymous expressions central to stylistics, Beardsley finds it quite irrelevant; indeed, he believes the concept of synonymy to be invalid. Beardsley's two-fold thesis is "that style is detail of implicit meaning" and that "good style is logical congruity of explicit and implicit meaning."

RECENTLY I had occasion to look over a couple of manuscripts that had been pretty heavily copy-edited for the press. The copy-editors had very different suggestions about the ideal direction in which to mould the hapless works that had come their way, but one thing they did thoroughly agree upon: namely, that the authors did not know how to write, and would be helpless without an editor. The main trouble was apparently not grammar or punctuation or consistency of capitalization, but style.

Reading these manuscripts, comparing the harshly cancelled original sentences with the neatly written substitutes between the lines, led me to reflect again on the puzzling nature of style—a quality so evident to the sensitive reader, and yet so difficult to lay hold of and to talk sensibly about. It brought home to me the paradox of the situation in which one person undertakes to improve the style of something written by another. *A* writes his piece of discursive prose, and shows it to *B*. *B*, the style-improver, may be a copy-editor or a teacher correcting a composition by a student, or may even be *A* himself at some later time. How is it possible for *B* to improve *A's* work? It can't be that *A* has failed to say what he wanted to say, because if he hasn't said it, how does *B* know what it is? And if *A has* said what he wanted to say, what can be wrong with the style?

Whether or not this is a real paradox, and, if so, how deep it goes, is one of the questions that I shall be trying to answer. Evidently it calls for a careful consideration of the nature of style: what style is precisely, and what

From *Reflections on High School English: NDEA Institute Lectures 1965*, ed. Gary Tate (Tulsa: University of Tulsa, 1966), pp. 91–105. With revisions, June, 1966. Reprinted by permission of Gary Tate and the author.

it means to change the style of a sentence or a paragraph.

It's just as well for us to recognize at the start that there are several very different concepts of style, or uses of the term. I will distinguish the three main ones briefly, so as to get my bearings.

First, there is the concept of *a* style (that is, the distinctive style of an author or a particular work). When we think of *a* style, in this sense, we have in mind, no doubt, certain recurrent features of the writing. A style is a set of stylistic features. To escape a futile circularity in this definition, we must go on to say what a stylistic feature is—that is, what features of a discourse count as elements of style, and which do not.

Second, there is the concept a *good style*. The style-improver claims to make the style better, and presumably is guided by some criteria of evaluation. He must be able to say what is a fault of style, and why it is a fault, and how that fault can be eliminated—without creating some other fault.

Third, there is the concept of style itself—a part or aspect of the discourse, somehow distinguishable from what is called the substance or content.

The first concept will not concern us here; it is of aesthetic interest and importance, but we can set it aside. My chief attention will be on the second concept. My aim is to look at certain problems about style from the point of view of the style-improver—especially of the teacher who hopes not only to improve particular pieces of work by his students, but also to give them some guiding principles, or at least teach them a knack, so that they may become, as far as may be, their own style-critics.

Because of the special point of view I am adopting, I feel free to use the term "good style" in a modest way. When I speak of good style in this context I do not mean excellence or distinction—style that can claim special aesthetic merit. I mean only *not-bad style*, that is, style that is free of faults. It may seem over-generous to award this commendation to what may, at its best, pass un-noticed; but I think experienced teachers will agree with me that to achieve good style, even in the modest sense, is no mean feat. And it is not a modest ambition for a teacher or copy-editor to set himself the task of eliminat-ing stylistic faults or helping others eliminate the faults in their own writing.

But in order to inquire what good style, or better style, is, I must lay the groundwork by giving, in summary, my answer to the third, and most fundamental question: what is style itself?[1] There are, then, three parts to my discourse: I shall consider what style is, and what good (or better) style is, and I shall discuss some of the practical consequences.

I

Many charming, clever, and memorable things have been said about style—most of which turn out to be highly misleading when subjected to analysis. One of

[1] The view sketched here has been formulated more precisely and fully in my *Aesthetics: Problems in the Philosophy of Criticism* (New York: Harcourt, Brace and World, 1958), pp. 221-27. It comes essen-tially from William K. Wimsatt; how much I have learned from, and relied upon, him will be evident to anyone who has read his essay on "Style as Meaning" in *The Prose Style of Samuel Johnson* (New Haven: Yale University, 1941; paperbound 1963).

the best things was said by Pascal, in his twenty-third
Pensée, and I would like to take it as my text: "Words
differently arranged have a different meaning, and meanings differently arranged have different effects."[2] When
this double-barrelled aphorism is properly understood
(that is, when I have gotten through telling you how *I*
want to construe it), it sums up concisely the two theses
I shall defend here, and it contains the two truths (the
only two really general and fundamental truths) about
style. Anyone who grasps their implications, and follows
them out consistently in practice, will find that the consequences are far-reaching.

The clearest way to say what style is, I think, is to say
what a *difference* in style is. Take two sentences or parts
of sentences, S_1 and S_2. We say that they differ in style
when two things are true about them. First, they differ
to some extent in *meaning*. And second, the difference is
not on the plane of overt or explicit meaning, but on the
plane of covert or implicit meaning. The distinction
between explicit and implicit meaning is one that requires a certain amount of analysis to elucidate, but let
me make it roughly, and leave it for the examples to
sharpen. Implicit meaning includes what we would
ascribe to the connotations rather than to the plain
dictionary sense of a word, and it includes what we
would consider to be merely suggested, or hinted, or
intimated by a sentence rather than what the sentence
plainly states.

It is relatively easy to see what we are talking about
when we compare two similar English expressions with
respect to their style. If they don't differ at all in meaning, there is no difference in style (but this, as Pascal

[2] Trans. W. F. Trotter (New York: Modern Library, 1941), p. 11.

says, is almost impossible, for if there are different words, or the same words in a different order, there is almost certain to be some difference in meaning, however small and subtle). If the meanings differ in some explicit way, there is no difference in style. It follows from this analysis that the concept of style is inherently comparative, and therefore variable with the context of concern. To isolate a particular stylistic feature in any discourse is always to think of a particular element of implicit meaning in terms of which that discourse might differ from some other one. This is the first of my two theses, then: that style is detail of implicit meaning.

To clarify and support this thesis I require a few examples. And I will take them from a book on style that is regarded by many people with great affection and respect—the E. B. White revision of William Strunk, Jr.'s *The Elements of Style*.[3] I'm not choosing this as a bad example; when I speak critically of it, I do so more in sorrow than in anger. I can only say: what a pity that even so sound and sensible a book is so confused! In the final chapter, contributed by White, the view of style I have been sketching above is clearly stated and subscribed to: "Style has no such separate entity; it is non-detachable, unfilterable" (p. 55)—in other words, it is inseparable from meaning. But unfortunately the logical implications of this thesis are seldom kept in view.

Consider first the advice to use the active voice rather than the passive voice or constructions based on the verb "to be." "Many a tame sentence of description or exposition," say Strunk and White (p. 14), "can be made lively and emphatic by substituting a transitive in the active voice for some such perfunctory expression as

[3] New York: Macmillan, 1959.

there is, or *could be heard."* Here is a clear-cut example of stylistic advice: how to make your sentence more lively and emphatic. Now take a look at some of their examples. The first one is this: Don't say "There were a great number of dead leaves lying on the ground;" but say "Dead leaves covered the ground." Granted there is a significant difference in style here. But isn't that a difference of meaning? For one thing, there are more leaves in the second sentence. The second one says that the ground was covered; the first one only speaks of a "great number." Stylistic advice is a rather odd sort of thing if it consists in telling students to pile up the leaves in their descriptions. Suppose the student brings the corrected paper back to his instructor and says, "Pardon me. You told me to say the leaves covered the ground, but actually they didn't; there was quite a bit of ground showing through. Still, there *were* a great many. Do I get a lower grade just for telling the truth?" What answer can the conscientious style-expert give to that?

Now, you may say, well it's not as if the student had used an exact number. Suppose he wrote, "There were 261 leaves on the ground," and his instructor commented in the margin: "Don't say there were 261; say there were 893—that will be more effective." This would of course be telling the student to lie. Since this difference in meaning would be explicit, the change from 261 to 893 would not be a change in style. But isn't the change from "a great many leaves" to "covered the ground" a kind of lie, too—or at least a considerable exaggeration? Naturally it is more lively and emphatic, but is it honest? True, the deception will be partially concealed, because it is conveyed implicitly rather than explicitly, but that does not make it less reprehensible.

Take another example that Strunk and White use to illustrate the same rule about liveliness and emphasis. Don't say "The reason he left college was that his health became impaired;" say "Failing health compelled him to leave college." What's the difference here? Again, it is a difference in meaning—in the picture of the situation that is conjured up by the different words and different grammar. In the one case, the health grew worse, and finally after some indecision, he left college—though health was not necessarily the sole consideration. The second sentence implies worse health: it left the student no choice. Naturally it is a more dramatic story. But is this what stylistic advice is all about? Are Strunk and White saying, "Never mind about the exact truth; always try to make things as dramatic as possible, provided you don't get caught in any explicit and easily detectable misstatements"?

The same sort of question can be raised about a great many of the Strunk-White examples. "Put statements in a positive form," they urge—"Make definite assertions" (p. 14). For instance, don't say "He was not very often on time," but rather "He usually came late." Now it seems to me that if I were asked about so-and-so's punctuality I might very well reply, "He was not very often on time," if I wanted to be careful not to overstate the matter, or to suggest that so-and-so came *very* late, or that he was deliberate and inconsiderate in coming late, etc. I am saying precisely what I want to mean, and ought to mean. What right has anyone to tell me *not* to mean this?

One more example: "Use definite, specific, concrete language," say Strunk and White (p. 15). If you take this seriously, it means, "Don't write philosophy, because that will require abstract language." But here is one of their examples: don't say "A period of unfavorable weather set in;" say "It rained every day for a week." But this is like the leaves example; the second sentence gives us a higher rainfall.

My immediate purpose is not to question the advice given, though I suppose some of my skepticism has already emerged. I am coming to the question of good style shortly. My argument is that a difference of style is always a difference in meaning—though implicit—and an important and notable difference of style is always a sizeable difference in meaning. Some of the Strunk-White examples involve so considerable and obvious a change that it is questionable whether they are really stylistic changes. For example: don't say "He did not think that studying Latin was much use;" say "He thought the study of Latin useless" (p. 14). Now being useless (i.e., having no use at all), and not being of much use, are clearly different things. If anybody advised me to say the second after I had said the first, I would be rather annoyed—I would tell him not to go putting words in my mouth. I don't think that studying Latin is much use; but I would certainly not want to say that it is useless. I'm afraid our style-advisers got carried away on this one.

I can't resist one more example—this one not from Strunk and White but from a religious publication via the filler-spaces in *The New Yorker*.

Words that sound happy put your reader in the right frame of mind to say "yes" to your request. Remember that a negative word or an unfriendly expression should never be used if there is a positive way to express the same thought. You might say: "We regret that we are unable to supply you with the item ordered. Is there another item which we may send you on the same subject?"

But your reader-reaction will be 100 per cent improved if you rephrase that sentence to read: "Fortunately for you, although the specific item you ordered is out of print, we have another which might serve your purpose."

Nothing could be plainer than that this change of style is a radical change in meaning. None of us would countenance such a bland invitation to write "words that sound happy" in order to con the subnormal reader into the appropriate "reader-reaction"—so that he gets the impression that you are practically doing him a favor by not sending him the item he ordered. But we encourage this sort of confusion when we speak of style as though it *were* detachable and manipulable independent of meaning—when we define style as the "how" of writing vs. the "what"—when, in short, we lose sight of the fact that style is nothing but meaning. That is what encourages people to entertain so absurd an idea as that there is both a "positive" and a "negative . . . way to express the same thought."

II

Now, if we are agreed about what style is, we can go on to the second question: what is *good* (i.e., not-bad) style? I assume that there are such things as *faults* of style—or at least there are pieces of discourse that are faulty *in* style—and so the basic question is what such a fault may be. Then the absence of such faults will be goodness of style.

There is one sort of problem about good style that I want to make sure we set aside here. A person who accepted a dinner invitation at the White House in a

long Faulknerian sentence, or who wrote a letter of con-
dolence in early Hemingwayese, has no doubt committed some sort of error involving style. The error is not
an error *of* style, I think, but an error in the choice of
style; the result is not bad style, necessarily, but *inappropriate* style. It is a lack of decorum. In fact, it is just the
sort of error that one might commit if he took some of
the Strunk and White advice too earnestly. "The latter
sentence [the one not recommended] is less direct, less
bold, and less concise," they say at one point (p. 13). But
what kind of reason is this? In effect, they are saying,
"Always write so as to *appear* like a bold, decisive, forthright sort of person. Never mind how you actually feel,
or what the occasion is; just act bold."

What I am concerned with, then, is stylistic fault, and
again I take my cue from Pascal. "Meanings differently
arranged have different effects"—or, as I should put it,
when meanings are combined, some combinations are
better than others. But there are different ways of being
better. When explicit meanings are wrongly combined,
you get a logical fault (this is oversimplifying somewhat,
but take it as a first approximation). The trouble with a
sentence like "He married his widow's younger sister" is
that it describes a logical impossibility. There's nothing
wrong with the style. Freedom from logical error is good
logic—though of course it may not be great cogency. But
suppose explicit meanings are badly combined with
implicit meanings. Then we have a fault of style. My
second thesis is that such a fault is also a logical fault,
though its locus is different from ordinary explicit logical
error. In short, good style is logical congruity of explicit
and implicit meaning. When what a sentence suggests
or hints, and what its words connote, bear out the im-

plications of the explicit meaning of the sentence, we have no fault of style; but when there is a clash, something must be remedied. And since we take the explicit meaning as primary, we think of the implicit meaning as what requires to be altered, so we say that the style is bad—just as we say that the hat is too small for the head, rather than that the head is too large for the hat.

As Wimsatt puts it (paperbound ed., p. 10), "Bad style is not a deviation of words from meaning, but a deviation of meaning from meaning."

To prove this thesis would be more of a task than I could undertake here—it is, in fact more of a task than anyone has ever undertaken. But a few examples will show how it can be supported, and you can test it further on your own favorite examples of horrible style.

My examples will come, again, from Strunk and White —and it is a tribute to their slim volume that it yields so many provocative examples. "Place the emphatic words of a sentence at the end," they advise at one point, in boldface italics (p. 26). "The proper place in the sentence for the word or group of words that the writer desires to make most prominent is usually the end." This puts the cart before the horse. It is not correct to say that the emphatic words of a sentence should be placed at the end; it is correct to say that whatever words *are* placed at the end of an English sentence will thereby be given emphasis. In all practical discussions of style, it is essential to distinguish two kinds of thing that can be said. They are related as the factual and the evaluative, the *is* and the *ought*.

The first kind of statement is what might be called a *stylistic fact*, or a rhetorical fact. For example, "Whatever you place at the end of a sentence will tend to be

emphasized." Or, "In general, the active voice carries
with it a tone of greater assurance and decisiveness than
the passive voice." Many inexperienced writers make
mistakes because they do not grasp these facts about the
very nature of English constructions. And the teacher
can help a great deal merely by pointing these things
out. "Look, by placing this at the end, you implicitly
claim that it is more important than what you put earlier.
Is this what you want to claim?" Or, "Look; here you use
the passive voice; the active voice would make the sentence more direct and forthright. Which do you prefer?"
In this way, a teacher sensitizes his students to stylistic
facts so that they become more and more aware of
exactly what they *are* saying, implicitly. But there is no
call for the Strunk-White imperative here. The instruction is in the conditional form, like instruction in
checkers, gardening, golf, or winemaking: "If you do
such-and-such, then such-and-such a meaning will result." Strunk and White's second sentence can be taken
in this conditional form.

So there are stylistic facts; are there also *stylistic rules,*
or recommendations? There may be, as I said, rules of
appropriateness: such-and-such is the accepted style for
a thank-you note. But what more can we say? What
reason can we give for condemning style, quite apart
from what the writer wished to do? Some of the Strunk-
White examples of poor style break down at once if we
suppose a different context. Take the first example under
the sentences just quoted. They reject this sentence:
"Humanity has hardly advanced in fortitude since that
time, though it has advanced in many other ways." They
substitute: "Humanity, since that time, has advanced in
many other ways, but it has hardly advanced in forti-

tude." Suppose you wrote the first sentence, and your copy-editor substituted the second one. Couldn't you simply reply that the first one says exactly what you want to say? From this reply there is no appeal. The second sentence, but not the first one, suggests that what is important is the lack of advance in fortitude. As far as style is concerned, one sentence is no better than the other; they simply say (implicitly) different things, and the question is (or ought to be) which is true.

But when Strunk and White condemn one sentence and praise the other, it is clear that they are making a hidden assumption. They are thinking of the sentence in the context of a sort of Baconian essay on the subject of fortitude. It's not easy to illustrate this assumption very briefly. But imagine something like this foreshortened context:

Man is a miracle, or many miracles; but the most miraculous fact about him is his fortitude, his capacity to endure and to survive incredible hardships. Think of the conditions under which neolithic man kept going—the winters, the wild animals, the long distances of his migrations. Humanity has hardly advanced in fortitude since that time, though it has advanced in many other ways.

Here if we feel a slackness at the end, and a sort of betrayal of expectations, we can affirm a fault of style. For the end of the last sentence implicitly denies what the first sentence quite explicitly states: namely, that fortitude is the important topic under discussion. So there is a logical conflict after all, and this is the stylistic fault. Note that it is quite independent of the writer's intention and the reader's antecedent desires: it is internal to the discourse itself.

Compare another example that illustrates the same principle, though Strunk and White place it under the heading of active vs. passive voice. They cite: "I shall always remember my first visit to Boston," and continue "This is much better than 'My first visit to Boston will always be remembered by me'" (p. 13). But what's wrong with the latter sentence? If we look for the relevant stylistic fact, we find that it is the same one just considered. Putting the personal pronoun at the end rather than at the beginning of the sentence gives it an emphatic position, and the emphasis is increased by the unusual syntax. Compare these two analogous sentences:

(1) The police department will always remember my first visit to Boston.

(2) My first visit to Boston will always be remembered by the police department.

It would be silly to say that in this case the passive voice makes the second sentence "less direct, less bold, and less concise." I suppose it is less direct, but it is more dramatic and striking, because of its ominous overtones.

So it is not the active-passive difference that is important here. The difference is that the second sentence given by Strunk and White ("My first visit to Boston will always be remembered by me") implicitly claims that there is something noteworthy about *my* remembering it, as opposed to somebody else's remembering it. It says, in effect, "Others may forget it, but *I* certainly won't." Now this suggestion in itself can't make the sentence stylistically bad. One could invent a context in which it would be better than the sentence Strunk and White recommend. But they are tacitly thinking of it as in a context where the main topic under discussion has been, or is to be, the trip itself, its causes and consequences. And in *this* context, the implicit suggestion that there is something significant about *my* remembering it rather than somebody else introduces an irrelevant point. In effect, the sentence says, "It is important that *I* remember it," but the context shows that it is *not* important, because it has no logical bearing upon the other matters at hand.

At one point in their book, Strunk and White come close to making this point explicitly. They begin unpromisingly by giving advice that verges upon complete nullity. First they state their rule: "Use the active voice" (p. 13)—just like that, in so many words. But a little later they say, "This rule does not, of course, mean that the writer should entirely discard the passive voice, which is frequently convenient and sometimes necessary." All we need now is some explanation of how to tell when it is convenient and when necessary—but the much-praised conciseness of *The Elements of Style* naturally prevents them from pausing to give any such explanation. However, their example and comment are important. Compare "The dramatists of the Restoration are little esteemed today" with "Modern readers have little esteem for the dramatists of the Restoration." The authors add, "The first would be the preferred form in a paragraph on the dramatists of the Restoration; the second, in a paragraph on the tastes of modern readers." Excellent; right to the point. The difference in style is a difference in what is suggested about the focus of attention in the whole discourse. And the rightness or wrongness of the style depends on how that suggestion actually comports with the remainder of the discourse.

Some people may be puzzled by this sort of talk about

style. In order to show what style is, and what good style is, you have to work out the implicit meanings and state them baldly for examination. Then they are no longer implicit, of course, and the explication of them may seem forced and artificial. But implicit meanings can be understood and can be stated explicitly; and that is the only way to exhibit their connections or divergences. This is what I call style-analysis. And it is essential if our discussions of style are not to degenerate into murky rhapsody or painfully misleading aphorism.

Perhaps I am stacking the cards too much for my second thesis by choosing examples that have already been selected, or constructed, to illustrate particular stylistic faults. So let me venture out of the laboratory for a brief field trip in the outside world of prose. My first specimen is one that came to hand not long ago in a book review by Elizabeth Janeway. She referred to the author of this book[4] as "a mistress of nearly impenetrable prose," and offered the following sample:

The tyranny of happiness forms the nucleus of the defense apparatus employed by the woman who does not quite dare to break out, though restless, but who must continually seek a validation for her way of life.

Now granted this would be much clearer if we had a context in which "the tyranny of happiness" was defined. But even with that explanation on hand, there would still be stylistic trouble. And that comes largely because the connotations of the words are constantly working against the basic logical pattern proposed by the very same words. They are also working against each other.

We are told that the woman does not "dare to break

[4] Edith de Rham, *The Love Fraud* (New York: Clarkson N. Potter, 1965); see *The New York Times,* March 28, 1965.

out" of something (I suppose, the frustrations of her second-class status as married woman); she is compelled to "seek a validation" for her way of life. So far, so good, though we could follow the logical order of relationships better if the sequence of phrases in the sentence reflected that order. The next step—which would be clearer if it followed rather than preceded the end of the sentence— is to note that in order to find that validation, the woman requires a "defense apparatus." But "defense" is hardly the *mot juste* here, since it suggests some sort of enemy or attack, and leads us to look around in the context for hints as to what it is—only to return empty-handed. Then the "defense apparatus" is said to have a "nucleus," and again we try to fit the connotations into the picture—if there is a nucleus it holds things together, or is the center, or is surrounded by other material, etc. No apparatus that is readily conceivable has, in the strict sense, a nucleus—though it may have a most important part. Finally (but this is put first), the nucleus is said to be formed by the tyranny of happiness. Is it the tyranny itself, or the acceptance of such tyranny, or some theory about such tyranny, or something else, that the woman relies on for her validation? The syntax, apparently elliptical, claims a causal connection that is unwarranted by the rest of the context, as far as we have it here. And that is the secret of its failure—as style.

It is always interesting, and often instructive, to see what reviewers pick out as objectionable in the style of the books they review. Recently Joseph Epstein, reviewing a book[5] in the *New Republic* (June 5, 1965), wrote:

Although every so often Coser will get off a cleanly barbaric sentence like "Geographical dispersion shades into or over-

[5] Lewis Coser, *Men of Ideas* (New York: Free Press, 1965).

laps with functional differentiation," he occasionally achieves a graceful prose style and almost always commands a forceful one.

This example suggests many reflections—more than I will try to tease out now. It is just the sort of sentence of which Strunk and White would be likely to say: "Avoid abstract nouns. Be concrete. Be definite. Be forceful." But the trouble does not lie in the abstract nouns, I think, and they would not even obtrude on our attention if it weren't for the *active* and *concrete* verbs between them—namely "shades into" and "overlaps with." It is the connotations of these words that throw us off and leave us baffled when we try to figure out what is the exact relationship between geographical dispersion and functional differentiation that is being asserted.

Last week, in a hotel in Denver, I found a booklet containing information about restaurants and other tourist attractions.[6] One of the items read as follows:

LE PROFIL—1560 Sherman St. (222-0758).
Richly adorned and unique of its kind, here dinner is an experience. French and Continental cuisine with an air of Paris sophistication is skillfully prepared and served with care. This is truly a swish dining emporium. The atmosphere is relaxed but polished.

I'm sure any composition teacher would itch to get at this piece of prose; it exhibits such a fascinating range of defects. But I pass by the dubiously attached modifier and the curious redundancy in the first sentence, and what philosophers would call a "category mistake" in the second sentence (I mean that it is not strictly the cuisine but the food that is served). These certainly introduce meanings that distract from the basic order of thought—

---

[6] *Colorado Guestguide,* Vol. 7, 1965 summer edition, p. 8.

they strew logical red herrings along the path of sense. But my favorite sentence is the third. "Truly a swish dining emporium"! It would be hard to find two words whose connotations—whose whole ambiances of meaning—are more at odds with one another.

III

I promised some concluding remarks on practical applications, but as I look back it seems to me that I have drawn the practical consequences pretty much as I went along. However, it may be well to summarize my argument concisely, and take one more look to see whether other useful points emerge.

The steps of my argument are these. (1) Different words or a different order of words make different meanings—at least, they do if they make a difference in style, because style is detail of implicit meaning. (2) Therefore, if the teacher advises a change of words, or of word order, he is recommending a different meaning. And if he says one stylistic feature is better than another, he is saying that it is better to mean one thing rather than another. (3) No meaning as such is better than any other, considered solely from the stylistic point of view. (Of course there are moral and political and religious and other criteria of what we ought to mean.) (4) Therefore, if a change of meaning betters the style, that betterment must lie in the relationships of meanings. (5) The objective relationships that meanings have to each other are logical; meanings are compatible or incompatible, they are connected by causation, implication, coordination, subordination, etc. (6) Therefore, faults of style must be faults of logic; and good style must be compatibility of implicit and explicit meaning.

The practical problem for the writer is that of managing his implicit meanings so that they do not impede or divert or conceal or obstruct his explicit meanings. It is a continuous tactical problem. The strategy of writing is large-scale organization of meanings—the main steps of the argument, explicit logical relationships. What is left is management of the small-scale, subtler, and under-the-surface meanings to make them carry the thought forward, adding details on the side (so to speak), but details that fit in and enrich the thought—and perhaps show how the writer looks upon his own argument: how confident or doubtful he is, how detached or involved, how serious or playful, and so on.

A teacher who fully realizes that to change style is always to change meaning will never take his role as style-critic lightly, I think. He will shy away from simple absolute rules. He will not speculate about intentions, but focus on the discourse itself, and the way its parts work, or do not work, together. His main effort will be to help his pupils understand what I have called stylistic facts, so that they can become sensitive and discerning readers of their own work. And above all when he is faced with a hard writing-problem, he will insist that the sovereign remedy is to think out the logical connections clearly, and then make sure that the syntax and diction mirror those connections as clearly as possible.

I think I have time to play around with one final example from Strunk and White—or rather from White's concluding chapter—and to draw another moral from it. The moral (to state it first) is that the doctrine of style as meaning and of good style as logical relevance has a liberating effect on the style-critic (the teacher or copy-editor); if he really accepts the doctrine, and all its consequences, he should become tolerant of very differ-

ent styles and undictatorial about his own recommendations.

White has some fun with variations on Thomas Paine:
"These are the times that try men's souls." And the last
and most outrageous variation is this: "Soulwise, these
are trying times." White raises the question what is
wrong with this—but he wisely makes no attempt to
answer this question. Less wisely, no doubt, I rush in to
fill the gap. Because it may seem that here, at any rate,
is a stylistically bad sentence whose stylistic badness has
nothing to do with logic, and therefore a sentence that
can be rejected out of hand without taking into account
relationships of meaning at all. Now of course, this sentence is a comedown from the original, and we can see
how it differs and why it differs. "Trying times" and
"times that try men's souls" are far from synonymous—
a situation can be trying, in the modern sense, without
constituting a real trial of one's whole self. And the
"X-wise" construction has taken on foundation-board and
executive-level overtones, besides its native vagueness
and indeterminateness. "Soulwise, these are trying times"
is flippant in tone, not deeply concerned. It reminds me
of a crazy line from an S. J. Perelman television script:
"A man in my position doesn't have as much freedom,
choicewise."

But now suppose young Tom Paine were to bring you
the first installment of a political piece he is writing,
called *The American Crisis*. You open it up and read the
first sentence: "Soulwise, these are trying times." Somehow it won't do. But what can you tell him? First, you
can help him see the relevant stylistic facts, so that he
knows exactly what he has said, explicitly and implicitly.
You cannot prove to him, I think, that his sentence in

itself is bad style. It might make an excellent beginning of a piece by Perelman. But, second, you can ask what kind of book this sentence is to be the beginning of— you can read further into the context. If the next sentence says, explicitly, that these times are not for the summer soldier and the sunshine patriot, but call for deep commitment and solemn purpose, then you can tell him that, in this context, the first sentence is bad style. For it says, implicitly, that the situation is not serious and that the writer does not care deeply about what is happening.

Let us suppose that, armed with this new insight, Tom Paine goes away to meditate. If you have helped him discern the logical jarring in his discourse, and have made him want to eliminate it, you have done your job. The rest is up to him. But of course if he returns the next day saying, "I've got it! Listen to this: 'These are the times that try men's souls,'" then you can congratulate yourself, as well as him. Unfortunately, few of our students are likely to come up to this level. So we had better be content with the more limited purpose of showing what is wrong, and why. But—and this is my parting plea—when we give reasons to argue that the style is faulty, let us make sure that we give *good* reasons. For bad reasons are worse than none at all.

Persuasive Definitions (Parts I-II)

CHARLES L. STEVENSON

Charles L. Stevenson (1908-   ) was born in Ohio and educated at Yale, Cambridge, and Harvard Universities, and has taught at Harvard, Yale, and the University of Michigan, where he is now professor of philosophy. Among his works are *Ethics and Language* (1944) and *Facts and Values* (1963). Although Stevenson is, like Beardsley, primarily a philosopher—his chief interests are ethics and aesthetics— one of his most important contributions to philosophy is also an important contribution to rhetoric: the concept of persuasive definition. A persuasive definition is an effective, because very persuasive, choice among synonymous expressions; its purpose is not to clarify discourse, the usual purpose of a definition, but to redirect attitudes, to change people's minds.

A "PERSUASIVE" definition is one which gives a new conceptual meaning to a familiar word without substantially changing its emotive meaning, and which is used with the conscious or unconscious purpose of changing, by this means, the direction of people's interests.

The object of this paper is to show that persuasive definitions are often used in philosophy, and that the widespread failure to recognize them for what they are—the temptation to consider them as definitions which merely abbreviate, or which analyse, common concepts—has led to important philosophical confusions.

Before considering philosophical examples, however, it will be helpful to consider some simpler ones, which will serve to make clearer what persuasive definitions are.

As an initial example let us take a definition of the word "culture". It will be convenient to invent pure fictions about the linguistic habits of the people to whom the definition is addressed; for this will typify the actual situation in a way that is free from complicating irrelevancies. Let us consider, then, a hypothetical community in which "culture" began by having an almost purely conceptual meaning. Let us sketch the development of its emotive meaning, show why the emotive meaning led certain people to redefine the word, and examine the way in which this redefinition achieved its purpose.

There was once a community in which "cultured" meant *widely read and acquainted with the arts*.

In the course of time these qualities came into high favour. If one man wanted to pay another a compliment, he would dwell at length upon his culture. It became unnatural to use "culture" in any but a laudatory tone of

From *Mind*, XLVII (July, 1938), 331–338. Reprinted by permission of *Mind* and the author.

voice. Those who lacked culture used the word with awe, and those who possessed it used the word with self-satisfaction, or perhaps with careful modesty. In this way the word acquired a strong emotive meaning. It awakened feelings not only because of its conceptual meaning, but more directly, in its own right; for it recalled the gestures, smiles, and tone of voice which so habitually accompanied it. A public speaker, for instance, was never introduced as "a man widely read and acquainted with the arts". He was described, rather, as "a man of culture". The latter phrase had no different conceptual meaning than the former, but was more suitable for awakening in the audience a favourable attitude.

As the emotive meaning of the word grew more pronounced, the conceptual meaning grew more vague. This was inevitable, for emotive meaning made the word suitable for use in metaphors. Men who were not cultured, literally, were often called so, particularly when they were admired for having *some* of the defining qualities of "culture". At first people readily distinguished these metaphorical compliments from literal statements; but as the metaphors grew more frequent, the distinction became less clear. People weren't quite sure whether a person *must* know about the arts in order to be literally cultured. Perhaps some other kind of knowledge would serve as a substitute.

Let us now suppose that one member of the community had no wholehearted regard for mere reading, or mere acquaintance with the arts, but valued them only to the extent that they served to develop imaginative sensitivity. He felt that they were not always a reliable means to that end, and on no account the only means. It was his constant source of regret that such mechanical procedures as reading, or visiting museums, should win instant praise, and that sensitivity should scarcely be noticed. For this reason he proceeded to give "culture" a new meaning. "I know", he insisted, "that so and so is widely read, and acquainted with the arts; but what has that to do with culture? The real meaning of 'culture', the true meaning of 'culture', is *imaginative sensitivity*." He persisted in this statement, in spite of the fact that "culture" had never before been used in exactly this sense.

It will now be obvious that this definition was no mere abbreviation; nor was it intended as an analysis of a common concept. Its purpose, rather, was to redirect people's interests. "Culture" had and would continue to have a laudatory emotive meaning. The definition urged people to stop using the laudatory term to refer to reading and the arts, and to use it, instead, to mean imaginative sensitivity. In this manner it sought to place the former qualities in a poor light, and the latter in a fine one, and thus to redirect people's admiration. When people learn to call something by a name rich in pleasant associations, they more readily admire it; and when they learn not to call it by such a name, they less readily admire it. The definition made use of this fact. It changed interests by changing names.

The past history of "culture" facilitated the change. The emotive meaning of the word, it is true, had grown up because of the old conceptual meaning; but it was now so firmly established that it would persist even though the conceptual meaning were somewhat altered. The old conceptual meaning was easily altered, since it had been made vague by metaphorical usage. The definition could effect a change in conceptual meaning, then, which left the emotive meaning unaltered. Thanks again to vagueness, the change seemed a "natural" one, which, by escaping the attention of the hearers, did not remind them that they were being influenced, and so did not stultify them by making them self-conscious. The effectiveness of the definition lay partly in this, and partly in the fact that it made its results permanent by embedding them in people's very linguistic habits.

The definition may be called "persuasive", then, in a quite conventional sense. Like most persuasive definitions, it was in fact doubly persuasive. It at once dissuaded people from indiscriminately admiring one set of qualities (wide reading and acquaintance with the arts) and induced them to admire another (imaginative sensitivity). The speaker wished to attain both of these ends, and was enabled, by his definition, to work for both at the same time.

There are hundreds of words which, like "culture", have both a vague conceptual meaning and a rich emotive meaning. The conceptual meaning of them all is subject to constant redefinition. The words are prizes which each man seeks to bestow on the qualities of his own choice.

In the nineteenth century, for instance, critics sometimes remarked that Alexander Pope was "not a poet". The foolish reply would be, "It's a mere matter of definition". It is indeed a matter of definition, but not a "mere" one. The word "poet" was used in an extremely narrow sense. This, so far from being idle, had important consequences; it enabled the critics to deny to Pope a laudatory name, and so to induce people to disregard him. A persuasive definition, tacitly employed, was at work in redirecting interests. Those who wish to decide whether Pope was a poet must decide whether they will yield to the critics' influence—whether they will come to dislike Pope enough to allow him to be deprived of an honorary title. This decision will require a knowledge of Pope's works and a knowledge of their own minds. Such are the important matters which lie behind the acceptance of the tacitly proposed, narrow definition of "poet". It is not a matter of "merely arbitrary" definition, then, nor is any persuasive definition "merely arbitrary", if this phrase is taken to imply "suitably decided by the flip of a coin".

Persuasive definitions are often recognisable from the words "real" or "true", employed in a metaphorical sense. The speaker in our first example, for instance, was telling us what "real" culture was, as distinct from the "shell" of culture. The following are additional examples: "Charity", in the true sense of the word, means the giving not merely of gold, but of understanding; true love is the communion between minds alone; "Courage", in the true sense, is strength against adverse public opinion. Each of these statements is a way of redirecting interests, by leaving the emotive meaning of the words unchanged, and wedding it to a new conceptual one. Similarly we may speak of the true meaning of "sportsmanship", "genius", "beauty", and so on. Or we may speak of the true meaning of "selfishness" or "hypocrisy", using persuasive definitions of these derogatory terms to blame, rather than to praise. "True", in such contexts, is obviously not used literally. Since people usually accept what they consider true, "true" comes to have the persuasive force of "to be accepted". This force is utilised in the metaphorical expression "true meaning". The hearer is induced to accept the new meaning which the speaker introduces.

Outside the confinements of philosophical theory the

importance of persuasive definitions has often been recognised. In philology they receive occasional stress. Or
rather, although little attention is given to persuasive
definitions, much is said about the broad heading under
which a study of them would fall: the interplay between
emotive and conceptual meanings in determining linguistic change, and its correlation with interests.

Leonard Bloomfield[1] presents us with a particularly
clear example: "The speculative builder has learned to
appeal to every weakness, including the sentimentality,
of the prospective buyer; he uses the speech forms whose
content will turn the hearer in the right direction. In
many locutions 'house' is the colorless, and 'home' the
sentimental word. Thus the salesman comes to use the
word 'home' for an empty shell that has never been
inhabited, and the rest of us follow his style."

Hanns Oertel, having stated that "the emotional element greatly influences the fate of some words", points
out that "amica" came to have one sense which was
synonymous with "concubina".[2] To be sure there are
several reasons for this. "Concubina" had become slightly
profane, too strong for delicate ears. And "amica" permitted a convenient ambiguity. Any shocking thoughts
could always be ascribed to those who chose to understand the word in its less innocent sense. But a persuasive factor must also have been involved. Tact often
required people to refer to concubines without expressing contempt. The word "amica", which retained part
of its old laudatory emotive meaning in spite of its new
sense, was useful in making concubines appear less con-
temptible.

---

[1] *Language* (Henry Holt, N.Y., 1933), p. 442.
[2] *Lectures on the Study of Language* (Scribner's, N.Y., 1902),
pp. 304, 305.

Persuasive definitions are too frequently encountered, however, to have been noticed solely by the philologists. An extremely penetrating account, in spite of its cynical turn, is given by Aldous Huxley, in his *Eyeless in Gaza:*

"But if you want to be free, you've got to be a prisoner. It's the condition of freedom—true freedom."

"True freedom!" Anthony repeated in the parody of a clerical voice. "I always love that kind of argument. The contrary of a thing isn't the contrary; oh, dear me, no! It's the thing itself, but as it *truly* is. Ask any die-hard what conservatism is; he'll tell you it's *true* socialism. And the brewer's trade papers; they're full of articles about the beauty of true temperance. Ordinary temperance is just gross refusal to drink; but true temperance, *true* temperance is something much more refined. True temperance is a bottle of claret with each meal and three double whiskies after dinner . . .

"What's in a name?" Anthony went on. "The answer is, practically everything, if the name's a good one. Freedom's a marvellous name. That's why you're so anxious to make use of it. You think that, if you call imprisonment true freedom, people will be attracted to the prison. And the worst of it is you're quite right."

II

As has been intimated, the study of persuasive definitions falls under a much broader heading: the correlation between terminology and interests. This correlation is highly complicated. A few observations will serve to show that our account of persuasive definitions deals with a severely limited aspect of it.

A change in meaning may be either a cause or an effect of a change in interest; and persuasive definitions figure only when the change in meaning is a cause. When it is an effect, as when our growing disapproval of present conditions in Germany causes us to use "fascist" as an epithet, there is not in this situation itself any element of persuasion; although once the word has acquired its derogatory associations, it may be used in persuasion later on.

Our subject is still more limited in scope than this. We are concerned with *definitions* which change interests. And it is important to note that we are concerned only with *some* of these definitions. Many definitions which redirect interests are not persuasive. Interests tend to be redirected by *any* definition, so long as it at all changes the meaning of a term, or selects some one sense to the exclusion of others. When a scientist introduces a technical term, in no matter how detached a manner, he indicates his interest in what he names—his estimation of the importance of talking about it, or of predicting its occurrence—and he often leads his readers to have a similar interest. It would be quite misleading to call such definitions "persuasive". How, then, are they to be distinguished from persuasive definitions?

The distinction depends upon whether the term defined has a strong emotive meaning, and upon whether the speaker employs the emotively laden word with dynamic purposes—with the predominating *intention* of changing people's interests. Men sometimes say, "I do not care what word you use, so long as you make my distinction;" and again, "If you are not interested in my distinction, well and good; I shall confine my remarks to the limited set of people who are". Definitions given in such a spirit are not persuasive; for although they indicate the speaker's interests, and may happen to influence the hearer's interests, they do not utilise emotive meaning in a deliberate effort to sway interests.

Such a distinction is inconveniently stringent, however, and must be slightly qualified. When a definition is given mainly for the purposes of distinction or classification, when it is used to guide only those interests which (like *curiosity*) are involved in making the classification understood, and when it in no way suggests that this is *the one* legitimate sort of classification, then the definition will not be called persuasive. (This is not meant to imply that persuasive definitions are never used in scientific writings, nor that non-persuasive definitions are based on some rock foundation, nor that persuasive definitions are less respectable than others.)

We must now proceed to a further point. Persuasive definitions redirect interests by changing only the conceptual meaning of an emotively laden term, allowing the emotive meaning to remain roughly constant. Clearly, the opposite change is equally important and prevalent: the emotive meaning may be altered, the conceptual meaning remaining constant. This latter device is no less persuasive. In fact, the same persuasive force can often be obtained either by the one linguistic change or by the other. In our initial example of "culture", for instance, the speaker used a persuasive definition. He might equally well have reiterated statements such as this: "Culture is only fool's gold; the true metal is imaginative sensitivity". This procedure would have permitted "culture" to retain its old conceptual meaning, but would have tended to make its emotive meaning derogatory; and it would have added to the laudatory emotive meaning of "imaginative sensitivity". The same purpose would have been served in this way that was served by the persuasive definition. The qualities commonly referred to by "culture" would still be placed in a poor light, and imaginative sensitivity in a fine one; but this would have been effected by a change in emotive meaning, rather than in conceptual meaning.

Cases of this last sort must be excluded from our account of persuasive definitions. Although persuasive, they are not secured through definition, but rather by one's gestures and tone of voice, or by rhetorical devices such as similes and metaphors. It is expedient to restrict the word "definition" to cases where conceptual meaning alone is being determined, or where, at least, this aspect predominates. We must not forget, however, that many statements which change mainly the emotive meaning of words may, in a wider sense, be called "definitions"; and that they, no less than persuasive definitions in our strict sense, may easily be confused with statements that are not persuasive. (For example: "By 'conscience' is meant the voice of destiny.")

The remarks of the last several pages may be summarised as follows: Persuasive definitions, so far from explaining the whole interrelationship between terminology and interests, deal only with the cases where change in terminology *causes* change in interest, where emotive meaning and dynamic usage are involved, and where the terminological change is in conceptual meaning only.

There is one further clarifying remark that deserves mention. The redirection of people's interests obviously depends upon much more than emotive meaning. It depends as well upon dynamic usage: upon the vigour of the speaker, his gestures, his tone of voice, the cadence of his accompanying sentences, his figures of speech, and so on. It is further conditioned by the temperament of the hearers, their respect for the speaker, their susceptibility to suggestion, their latent prejudices

and ideals—and indeed, by their factual beliefs, for a
sudden change in men's beliefs prepares the way
(though often with a "lag") for a redirection of interests.
Persuasion is seldom effective unless the hearers are
already on the point of changing their interests. A persuasive definition may then be important as a final
impetus to the change, and as a mnemonic device, im-
bedded in language, for keeping the change permanent.
In dwelling upon definitions, then, and upon the functions of emotive meaning, we have stressed but one
aspect of persuasive situations. There are excellent reasons for this stress, however. Emotive meaning is a fairly
stable element amid the widely varying set of factors
upon which effective persuasion depends, and although
a partial factor, is often essential. When a man redefines
an emotively laden term, moreover, he is *very* frequently
endeavouring to persuade, and takes care that the other
factors necessary to successful persuasion are fulfilled.
Emotive meaning is a reliable *sign* of persuasion—permits
it to be noticed. This is important in the case of definitions, where persuasion, however legitimate and vital in
itself, can so easily acquire a spurious appeal by masking
itself in the guise of a logical analysis.

U and Non-U:
An Essay in Sociological Linguistics

ALAN S. C. ROSS

Alan S. C. Ross (1907-   ) was born in England and educated at Oxford and Birmingham Universities, and has taught
at Leeds and Birmingham, where he is now professor of
linguistics. Among his many works are *Etymology with
Especial Reference to English* (1958) and *The Essentials of
Anglo-Saxon Grammar and Tables of Old English Sound
Changes* (1963). "U and Non-U: An Essay in Sociological
Linguistics" argues that some rhetorical choices—that is, some
choices among synonymous expressions—reveal to all upper-
class Englishmen, and to some middle- and lower-class Englishmen, whether the writer or speaker is upper class ("U")
or not upper class ("non-U") but that such choices, which
vary in effectiveness with the writer or speaker's purpose and
with his audience, are rarely free choices. A choice among
class dialects is a rhetorical choice. But it is a choice entailed
by one's choice of parents; and, unless one begins very early
to start to revoke a non-U choice (by going to a preparatory
school and then to a good public school), it is irrevocable.

TODAY, in 1955, the English class-system is essentially tripartite—there exist an upper, a middle, and a lower class. It is solely by its language that the upper class is clearly marked off from the others. In times past (e.g. in the Victorian and Edwardian periods) this was not the case. But, today, a member of the upper class is, for instance, not necessarily better educated, cleaner, or richer than someone not of this class. Nor, in general, is he likely to play a greater part in public affairs, be supported by other trades or professions,[1] or engage in other pursuits or pastimes than his fellow of another class. There are, it is true, still a few minor points of life which may serve to demarcate the upper class,[2] but they are

[1] It may, however, be doubted how far the Navy and the Diplomatic Service will in practice (in contradistinction to theory) be "democratised," even if there should be a succession of Labour Governments; foreigners seem to expect English diplomats to be of the upper class.

[2] In this article I use the terms *upper class* (abbreviated: U), *correct, proper, legitimate, appropriate* (sometimes also *possible*) and similar expressions (including some containing the word *should*) to designate usages of the upper class; their antonyms (*non-U, incorrect, not proper, not legitimate,* etc.) to designate usages which are not upper class. These terms are, of course, used factually and not in reprobation (indeed I may at this juncture emphasise a point which is doubtless obvious, namely that this whole article is purely factual). *Normal* means common both to U and non-U. I often use expressions such as *U-speaker* to denote a member of the upper class and, also, *gentleman,* pl. *gentlemen* (for brevity, in respect of either sex—the plural *gentlefolk* is no longer U). Class-distinction is very dear to the heart of the upper class and talk about it is hedged with taboo. Hence, as in sexual matters, a large number of circumlocutions is used. Forty years ago, as I understand, U-speakers made use of *lady* and *gentleman* without self-consciousness; the antonym of *gentleman* was often *cad* or *bounder*. Today, save by older people, these terms can hardly be used to indicate class-

From *Noblesse Oblige,* ed. Nancy Mitford (London: Hamish Hamilton Ltd., 1956). Reprinted by permission of Hamish Hamilton Ltd.

only minor ones. The games of real tennis and piquet,[3] an aversion to high tea, having one's cards[4] engraved (not printed), not playing tennis in braces, and, in some cases, a dislike of certain comparatively modern inventions such as the telephone, the cinema, and the wireless, are still perhaps marks of the upper class.[5] Again, when drunk, gentlemen often become amorous or maudlin or vomit in public, but they never become truculent.

In the present article I am concerned with the linguistic demarcation of the upper class. This subject has been but little investigated, though it is much discussed,

---

distinction, for they sound either pedantic or facetious (*you cad, Sir!*). *Lady* and *Gentleman* have, of course, senses quite unconnected with class-distinction, but, today, the use of these words in the sense "man" and "woman" between U-speakers has almost entirely vanished save when prefixed with *old* (*There's an old LADY to see you* is different from *There's an old WOMAN to see you*, for the former implies that the person is U, the latter that she is very non-U). *She's a nice lady* is non-U, *He's a nice gentleman* even more so (*man, woman,* or *girl* being the U-use here).

[3] But solo whist (or *solo* as its devotees call it) is non-U, though much "lower" games (e.g. pontoon, nap, and even Slippery Sam) are not necessarily so. Whist used to be a U-game but is, today, almost entirely confined to whist-drives, which are non-U (*they STAND UP to deal, my dear!*).

[4] The normal U-word is *card* (though this is ambiguous with (*playing*)-*card*). *Carte de visite* was apparently U but would today seem unbearably old-fashioned. *Calling-card* and *visiting-card* are non-U; the latter term is, in any case, an unfortunate one because of the non-U slang phrase *He's left his visiting-card* (of a dog)—foreigners would do well to beware of "idiomatic" sentences such as *The Picts left their visiting-card in the Pentland Firth* (said, in a public lecture, meaning that the name *Pict* is preserved in the first element of *Pentland*).

[5] Certainly many U-speakers hunt—but hunting has for long been something that the *nouveau riche* knows he should do in order to be U; many farmers hunt too. So, today, hunting is not *ipso facto* a class-indicator.

in an unscientific manner, by members of that class. The late Professor H. C. Wyld wrote a short article on the subject. He was well equipped for the task, for he was both a gentleman and a philologist. Today, his views are perhaps a little old-fashioned; for instance, the dictum "No gentleman goes on a bus," attributed to him, is one which most gentlemen have to neglect.

Both the written and the spoken language of the upper class serve to demarcate it, but the former to only a very slight extent. A piece of mathematics or a novel written by a member of the upper class is not likely to differ in any way from one written by a member of another class, except in so far as the novel contains conversation. In writing, it is, in fact, only modes of address, postal addresses, and habits of beginning and ending letters that serve to demarcate the class.

Before proceeding to the detail of the present study I must emphasise that I am here concerned only with usages which serve to demarcate the upper class. The line of demarcation relevant to this study is, often, a line between, on the one hand, gentlemen and, on the other, persons who, though not gentlemen, might at first sight appear, or would wish to appear, as such. Thus, habits of speech peculiar to the lower classes find no place here. I may also note here that the U-demarcation is of two types: (1) a certain U-feature has a different, non-U, counterpart, as non-U *wealthy* = U *rich*; (2) a certain feature is confined to U-speech and it has a counterpart which is not confined to non-U speech, e.g. the pronunciations of *girl* to rhyme with *hell* and *Hal* are U, but many (perhaps most male) U-speakers, like all non-U-speakers, use the pronunciation that rhymes with *curl*.

I. THE WRITTEN LANGUAGE

The following points may be considered:
(1) Names on envelopes, etc.
(2) Beginnings of letters.
(3) Names on cards.
(4) Postal addresses on envelopes, etc., at the heads of letters, and on cards.
(5) Letter-endings.

Of these points the first three are mutually linked and the second—beginnings of letters—is linked with the spoken language; for, in general, a person known to the writer is written to and spoken to in the same mode of address. It will therefore be convenient to treat all modes of address together, though this means taking the spoken modes out of place.

Modes of address, particularly those used for the nobility, have always been a bugbear to the non-U. It is, for instance, non-U to speak of an earl as *The Earl of P—*; he should be spoken of and to as *Lord P—* and also so addressed at the beginning of a letter if an introduction between him and the speaker/writer has been effected. If the acquaintance is close, *P—* should be used instead of *Lord P—*. Letters to baronets and knights to whom one has been introduced should begin *Dear Sir A— X—*[6] if the acquaintance is slight, *Dear Sir A—* if it is not slight. In speaking *to* one, only *Sir A—* is possible. In speaking *of* one, *Sir A—* should not be used unless the acquaintance is fairly close, *Sir A— X—*, or *X—*, being correct. If the acquaintance is slight or non-existent, the use of *Sir A—* in speaking of a baronet or knight is non-U

[6] *A—, B—, C—,* etc. are christian names (the initials being written *A., B., C.,* etc.); *X—* is a surname.

and "snobbish"[7] as attempting to raise the social tone
of the speaker. Letters to ambassadors whom one does
not know should begin *Dear Excellency* and the envel-
ope should be addressed *H.E. The P— Ambassador*. In
speech, a Lieutenant-Commander is addressed as *Com-
mander*, a Lieutenant in the Army as *Mister*. In concluding this section it may be noted that, in writing
letters to noblemen of very high rank, the rules laid
down in the etiquette-books[8] need not always be strictly
observed. Thus a Duke addressed by a stranger as *Dear
Sir* would not necessarily conclude that his correspond-
ent was non-U; he might be a left-wing gentleman with
a dislike of dukedoms.

On envelopes, gentlemen put *Esq.* after the names of
persons who are, or who might wish to be considered,
gentlemen, whether in fact armigerous or not. *Esq.* is,
however, not used of oneself, e.g. neither on a card
(which bears *Mr.*) nor on a stamped-and-addressed en-
velope enclosed for a reply (which has merely *A— B. X—*
or *A. B. X—* without prefix). Knowledge of at least one
initial of the recipient's name is, of course, a prerequisite

---

[7] "Snobs" are of two kinds; *true snobs* (Thackeray's kind) and
inverted snobs. Both kinds respect a person the more the better bred
he is. True snobs indicate this in their behaviour to, and in their conversation about, persons of good family, though they do not usually
admit this. In their conversation about (but not in their behaviour to)
such persons, inverted snobs indicate that they respect a person the
less the better bred he is. One would expect to find a third category:
those who really do respect a person the less the better bred he is,
and indicate it. But this third category does not appear to exist. Nearly
all English people are snobs of one of the two kinds (in this respect
England differs from Finland and Iceland and resembles Spain and
pre-War Hungary). And, just as it is impossible to find someone
exactly half male and half female, so it is impossible to find an English-
man in whom true and inverted snobbery exactly balance.

[8] It is, of course, very non-U actually to consult these.

for addressing him with *Esq.* If the writer has not this minimum knowledge (and cannot, or is too lazy to obtain it) he will be in a quandary. In these circumstances I myself use the Greek letter ☉ (as ☉. *Smith, Esq.*), but this is probably idiosyncratic. But to address someone as "—*Smith*," *Esq.* is not so much non-U as definitely rude.[9] Gentlemen usually address non-U males as *Mr.*; in internal circulation (e.g. in Government offices), gentlemen may address each other in this way. Schoolboys at their preparatory school (and younger boys) should be addressed as *Master*; at their public school, merely as *A. B. X*— (without prefix or suffix). The non-U usually address all adult males as *Mr.*, but tradespeople have copied the use of *Esq.* from their customers. Those gentlemen who are inverted snobs dislike *Esq.*, but, since they know that to address someone as *Mr.* is non-U, they avoid this also and address all adult males without prefix or suffix (like the correct mode of address for public-school boys). Intellectuals, of any class, often begin letters, even where the acquaintance is slight, with *Dear A— X—*.

Postal addresses. It is non-U to place the name of a house in inverted commas (as "*Fairmeads*") or to write the number in full, either without or (especially) with inverted commas (as *Two,*—worse "*Two,*"—*St. Patrick's Avenue*). The names of many houses are themselves non-U; the ideal U-address is *P— Q—, R—*, where *P—* is a place-name, *Q—* a describer, and *R—* the name (or abbreviation) of a county as *Shinwell Hall, Salop*.[10] But, today,

---

[9] I may note here that many U-speakers omit the *Esq.* on cheques.

[10] Here I may note a curious indicator. In speaking, it is, in general, non-U to use the whole name of such a house as in *I'm going to Shinwell Hall* (the U-sentence would be *I'm going to Shinwell*)—this obtains whether the house belongs to the speaker (or his relatives) or not.

few gentlemen can maintain this standard and they often live in houses with non-U names such as *Fairmeads* or *El Nido*.

Letter-endings. The U rules for ending letters are very strict; failure to observe them usually implies non-U-ness, sometimes only youth. In general, the endings of letters are conditioned by their beginnings. Thus a beginning (*Dear*) *Sir*[11] requires the ending *Yours faithfully*, unless the writer hopes to meet the recipient when *Yours very truly* may be used. Acquaintances who begin letters with *Dear Mr. X—* sign them *Yours sincerely* or *Yours very sincerely*; perversely, the latter ending is less cordial than the former. People who know each other really well will begin *Dear A—* or *Dear X—* (males only) and sign *Yours ever*. The ending *Yours* is often used even by gentlemen if they are in doubt as to which ending is appropriate.

The name after the letter-ending offers little scope for comment. Letters are perhaps most usually signed in such forms as *A— X—*, *A— B. X—*, *A. B— X—* (the choice between the two last depending upon which christian name the writer is normally called by). If the writer is unknown (or not well-known) to the recipient, the latter cannot know whether the former is plain *Mr.* (if male), *Miss*, *Mrs.*, or something else (if female); it is therefore usual for the writer to inform the recipient if he is other than plain *Mr.* (if male), other than *Miss* (if female). In handwritten letters, a usual way of doing this is to sign as, for instance, (*Professor*) *A— B. X—*; in type-written letters (*Professor A— B. X—*) may be typed below the handwritten signature *A— B. X—*. I have seen

[11] Whether the writer is U or not, this is the normal beginning of all business letters to unknowns; the variant *Sir* is correctly used to government officials, *Sire* (or *Your Majesty*) to kings; *My Dear Sir* is felt as American.

long titles (e.g. *Dowager Countess of*) appended as footnotes to the signature. In concluding this section I may mention that people sometimes sign themselves (or enter their names in lists, etc.) with the surname only; this usage is very non-U, the reason for its non-U-ness lying in the fact that the correct signature of peers is of this form (e.g. the Earl of *P—* signs himself just *P—*).[12]

Here I may refer to R. W. Chapman's excellent *Names, designations & appellations*, published in 1946.[13] The author states (p. 231) that the work is "an attempt to describe the modern use, in good society in this country, of personal names and designations, spoken or written, in the second or third person."[14] Chapman does not specifically deal with non-U usages but, since his enumeration is intended as exhaustive, it may be assumed that, essentially, usages divergent from those given by him are non-U, except in so far as I have dealt with them.

I may comment on certain points mentioned by Chapman where the usage of 1955 differs from that of a rather old-fashioned person writing some years earlier. I arrange the commentary by the pages of his book, either citing passages therefrom in inverted commas, or (where this would be too lengthy) indicating in square brackets [" "] the point under discussion.

pp. 237–8. ["Spouse: third person."] The mode in which a speaker refers to his spouse is markedly distinct

---

[12] The correct form of postcards differs slightly from that of letters, for both the beginning (*Dear A—*, etc.) and the ending (*Yours sincerely*, etc.) are omitted. Some U-speakers feel it wrong to sign a postcard to a friend by anything save the bare initial(s) (*A.* or *A. B. X.*).

[13] S. P. E. Tract No. XLVII.

[14] By the "second person" he means speaking *to* a person, by the "third person," speaking *of* one.

as between U- and non-U-speakers. A U-speaker, naming his wife to an equal, normally says *My wife* (or uses her christian name); to a very non-U person he says *Mrs. X—*. Chapman says (p. 237) of a U-speaker referring to the hearer's wife [" 'Your wife' may be over-familiar if I do not know Jones (i.e. the hearer) very well"]. He advocates the use, then, of *Mrs. Jones*. Actually, I think that, of recent years, there has been a considerable increase in the use of *Your wife, Your husband* by U-speakers, even in cases where the acquaintance is of the slightest. Non-U-speakers do not in general make use of *my/your wife/husband*, preferring *Mr./Mrs. X—*.

p. 238. [" 'What does Weston think of the weather?', Mr. Knightly asked Mrs. Weston. But I should be chary of following this precedent."]. I agree with Chapman. There is, however, rather a similar case, not mentioned by Chapman (doubtless because it is a very minor one) where surnames may be used. Schoolboys and young men frequently refer to each other by their surnames, so parents of a boy, talking to one of his acquaintances, often use the acquaintance's surname because they do not know his christian name; similarly, the acquaintance may call the son by his surname to the parents. It is not until a boy gets older (c. 16?) that he realises that he must deliberately ascertain his friends' christian names in order to be able to refer to them correctly to their parents. At Oxford in the late twenties the use of the surname in these circumstances was a known *gaucherie* and must therefore have been fairly usual.[15]

---

[15] In connection with surnames, I may mention a habit not noted by Chapman, *viz.* the abbreviation of the surnames of close friends. It was apparently U and was certainly thriving in the nineties; at a much earlier period it appears in Mrs. Henry Wood's *Johnny Ludlow* where

p. 240. [" 'Sir' is, of course, very often used between intimates with a slightly jocular or affectionate intention; one may say 'Good morning, Sir' to almost any intimate. 'My dear Sir, I am very glad to see you.' But 'My dear Sir' usually conveys a mild remonstrance."] These usages are, I think, obsolescent among U-speakers and young U-speakers are inclined to dislike them very much. In my experience people who use them are either non-U (very often, commercial travellers) or, if U, are elderly academics.

p. 241. ["The use of 'Sir' by young men to their seniors in general is not easily defined, and the practice varies."] This is certainly true; my own use is to reserve *Sir* for men of great age and/or great distinction. The War of 1939–45, like its predecessor of 1914–18, has brought about an enormous increase in the use of *Sir* because of Service rules. Chapman says ["Young women . . . are not expected to say *sir*"]—but now many do by reason of their having been in one of the women's Services.

p. 241. ["But is there any alternative (i.e. to *Miss*) if one is addressing a telephone operator or a barmaid?"] Yes, there is: silence, perhaps the most favourite of all U-usages today. Indeed it is remarkable how easy it is (save when engaged in activities such as bridge or poker) to avoid the use of any appellation at all.[16] This has become increasingly the practice of shyer gentlemen.

---

the young *Todhetley* is often called *Tod*. The custom is now obsolescent, save perhaps in the case of hyphenated surnames (*X-Y* may be called *X*) and between close women-friends (e.g. a *Miss Robinson* might be called *Robbie*).

[16] This U-habit of silence has had a curious corollary. Most nations say something when drinking (as *Skål* in Swedish or *Egészségére!* in Hungarian) but, until 1939, English U-speakers normally said nothing. Since then, however, the Service habit of saying something has become almost universal and most U-speakers therefore feel it churlish to say

The use of *Miss* in the circumstances mentioned by Chapman (and particularly to waitresses) is definitely non-U.

p. 243. ["Christian names."] On this matter, Chapman has a point of view out of date even by the early thirties. I can only just remember the time, in the very early twenties, when a typical boy-and-girl conversation might have run: *"He:* May I call you by your christian name? *She:* If you like. *He:* Er—what *is* your christian name?" Since that time the use of christian names by U-speakers has been continually increasing. In the thirties, it was quite customary for a member of a *partie carrée* going to a dance who was unknown to the other three to be introduced by the christian name alone (or, often, just as *John Smith* or *Jane Smith*, without prefix). In the War the use of christian names increased still further; in Government offices it was often the custom for a man at the head of a large section of girls to call them all by their christian names, while they called him *Mr. X—.*

p. 248. ["Use of surnames by women."] In the third person, it is now very usual for women to use the surname only of men (e.g. of their husbands' friends); for men, or women, to use the surnames only of women in this way is less common, though in some circles (e.g. university ones) it is quite accepted. In the second person, the use of the bare surname without christian name or prefix is rarer still. For a woman so to call a man is still either foreign, bohemian, or intellectual-left. In general, women call other women by the bare surname only in institutions for women (e.g. in girls' schools, women's colleges, hospitals, and, no doubt, in women's prisons).

---

nothing; repressing a shudder, they probably say *Cheers!* (though hardly *God bless!* which, though also frequent in the Services, seems non-U).

p. 250. ["Dukes: third person."] I may add that dukes, if fairly well known to the speaker, may appropriately be referred to by christian name and title, e.g. *George Birmingham*, meaning *George, etc., Duke of Birmingham.*

p. 251. ["A facetious use."] *His Lordship*, in facetious use, is definitely non-U and, often, inverted snob. There is a somewhat similar non-U expression: *young master* (as in *Young master's making himself quite at home!*) used of a young man considered "la-di-da" (for this word see below).

pp. 251, 255. ["Abbreviations."] *Honourable* and *Reverend* are abbreviated either as *Honble., Rev^d.* or as *Hon., Rev.* Both usages are quite U, though the former is the more old-fashioned.

p. 265. ["Some people say 'Miss Austen.'"] In my experience, to say *Miss Austen* instead of *Jane Austen* is either precious or pseudo-intellectual.

II. THE SPOKEN LANGUAGE

Pronunciation

(1) In a few cases, a difference of stress serves to demarcate a pronunciation as between U and non-U. Thus *yésterdáy* (with the same stress as *Wéstern Ísles*) is non-U as against U *yésterday*; or, again, U *témporarily* / non-U *temporárily*; U *fórmidable* / non-U *formídable*; U *ínt'resting* / non-U *interésting*; *Víenna* is old-fashioned U for normal *Viénna*; *cónfessor* and *súccessor* (like *Mass* to rhyme with *pass*, instead of *gas*) appear to be confined to Catholic U-speakers (these call themselves *Catholic* with first syllable to rhyme with

bath). In some cases two stress-variants may both be U as *spónge-cake* or *spónge-cáke* (non-U-speakers hardly use the word, substituting *sponge* for it).

(2) To pronounce words like *ride* as if spelt *raid* is non-U (*raid* was, however, undoubtedly Shakespeare's pronunciation of *ride*). This kind of pronunciation is often called *refained*.

(3) Many (but not all) U-speakers make *get* rhyme with *bit*, *just* (adverb) with *best*, *catch* with *fetch*.

(4) In U speech, *spoon* rhymes with *boon*, in non-U speech with the Yorkshire pronunciation of *bun*. Some U-speakers make *gone* rhyme with *born*.

(5) U-speakers do not sound the *l* in *golf*, *Ralph* (which rhymes with *safe*), *soldier*; some old-fashioned U-speakers do not sound it in *falcon*, *Malvern*, either, but it is doubtful how far this last survives.

(6) *Real*, *ideal* have two, respectively, three syllables in U speech, one, respectively, two in non-U speech (note, especially, non-U *really*, rhyming with *mealie*).

(7) *Fault*, *also*, *Balkans*, *Baltic*, *halt*, *malt*, *salt*, *vault* are pronounced by the U as if spelt *fawlt*, *awlso*, *bawlkans*, etc.

(8) In *Berkeley*, *Berkshire*, *clerk*, *Derby*, U-speakers rhyme the first syllable with *dark* (or *bar*), non-U speakers with *mirk* (or *burr*).[17]

(9) Some U-speakers pronounce *tyre* and *tar* identically (and so for many other words, such as *fire*—even going to the length of making *lion* rhyme with *barn*).

[17] Since it is definitely non-U to pronounce *Berkeley* with first syllable rhyming with *mirk*, U-speakers get a frisson if they have to enunciate the surnames *Birkley*, *Burkly* (correctly pronounced with first syllable rhyming with *mirk*) for, if a U-hearer does not appreciate the spelling of the names (rare ones), they may be suspected of using a non-U pronunciation.

(10) Miscellaneous words. (a) Acknowledge: U—
rhymes with *college* / non-U—2nd syllable rhymes with
bowl. *(b) Either*: U—1st syllable rhymes with *buy* /
non-U—1st syllable rhymes with *bee*. *(c) Forehead*: U—
rhymes with *torrid* / non-U—*fore-head*. *(d) Handker-
chief*: U—last syllable rhymes with *stiff* / non-U—last
syllable rhymes with *beef* or *weave*. *(e) Hotel* and
humour: to drop the *h* is old-fashioned U. *(f) Medicine*
and *Venison*: U—two syllables / non-U—three syllables.
(g) U *a nought* / non-U *an ought* (meaning "zero").
(h) Tortoise: U—pronounced identically with *taught
us* / non-U—last syllable rhymes with *boys* or *Boyce*.
(i) Vase: U—rhymes with *bars* / non-U—rhymes with
cause or *maize*. *(j)* W (the letter)[18]: U *double-you* /
non-U *dubby-you*.[19]

Vocabulary

Article (meaning "chamber-pot") is non-U; in so far
as the thing survives, U-speakers use *jerry* (a schoolboy
term) or *pot*.[20]

Bath. To TAKE *a bath* is non-U against U *to* HAVE *one's
bath*.

---

[18] *The* W is a frequent non-U expression for "the lavatory" (W.C.
is also non-U)—hence, no doubt, the non-U children's word *dubby* or
dub. (In this connection I may mention a U expression: *Let me show
you the* GEOGRAPHY *of the house* (meaning, essentially, the "lavatory").)

[19] Oddly enough, *Grammar* and *Syntax* (two very important philo-
logical domains) produce hardly any marks of class-difference. I have
noticed only (i) *I bought it at Woolworth* (without the final *'s*), a
usage confined to some U-speakers; (ii) the non-U use of the preposi-
tions in *He's* AT *boarding-school, She's* ON *holiday*; (iii) the North
country inversion in *He's been very decent, has John.*

[20] But the (recent?) transitive verb *to pot*, used of babies, is surely
non-U?

Civil: this word is used by U-speakers to approve the behaviour of a non-U person in that the latter has appreciated the difference between U and non-U, e.g. *The guard was certainly very civil.*

Coach (meaning "char-à-banc") is non-U, doubtless because the thing itself is. Those U-speakers who are forced, by penury, to use them call them *buses*, thereby causing great confusion (a *coach* runs into the country, a *bus* within a town).

non-U *corsets* / U *stays.*

Counterpane, bedspread, coverlet. Of these three synonyms, I think that the first is U, the second obsolete, the third non-U.

Cruet. The sentence *Pass the cruet, please* is very non-U; *cruets* are in themselves non-U. In gentlemen's houses there are, ideally, separate containers—*salt-cellars, pepper-pots* (*-castors, -grinders, -mills*) and *mustard-pots,* so that the corresponding U-expression will be *I wonder if you could pass the salt* (*pepper, mustard*), *please?* or the like. Vinegar is a fourth constituent of many cruets but many uses of vinegar (e.g. poured on fish or bacon-and-eggs) are definitely non-U.

Crust or crumb? used when cutting bread is (old-fashioned?) non-U.

Cultivated in *They're cultivated people* is non-U and so also is *cultured.* There is really no U-equivalent (some U-speakers use *civilised* in this sense).

Cup. How is your cup? is a non-U equivalent of *Have some more tea?* or the like. Possible negative non-U answers are *I'm doing nicely, thank you* and (*Quite*) *sufficient, thank you.* There is a well-known non-U affirmative answer: *I don't mind if I do* (but this was U about a century ago).

Cycle is non-U against U *bike, bicycle* (whether verb or noun); non-U *motorcycle* / U *motorbike, motorbicycle* is perhaps less pronouncedly so.

Dinner. U-speakers eat *lunch* in the middle of the day (*luncheon* is old-fashioned U) and *dinner* in the evening; if a U-speaker feels that what he is eating is a travesty of his dinner, he may appropriately call it *supper*. Non-U-speakers (also U-children and U-dogs), on the other hand, have their *dinner* in the middle of the day. *Evening meal* is non-U.

Dress-suit. This is a non-U word. A male U-speaker might answer the question *What shall I wear tonight?* in any of the following ways: (1) *Dinner jacket*; (2) *Short coat* (? old-fashioned); (3) *Black tie*; (4) *Tails*; (5) *White tie.* The term *evening dress* is often used on invitations but it has not a very wide currency among U-speakers (in any case, for men it is ambiguous); a sentence *Shall we wear evening dress?* would not be possible, the appropriate expression being *Are we going to change?*

Excuse my glove. This expression, used when shaking hands, is (? old-fashioned) non-U; male U-speakers do (used to ?) remove their glove in order to shake hands but say nothing.

Greatcoat (also *topcoat*?) are rather old-fashioned U, *overcoat* being normal. *Burberry*[21] and *raincoat* are of the same genre, *macintosh* or *mac* being normal.

Greens meaning "vegetables" is non-U.

Home: non-U *They've a lovely home* / U *They've a very nice house.*

---

[21] This use of *Burberry* no doubt arose because, even before 1914 (when U-speakers were richer than non-U-speakers), this was a good and expensive kind of macintosh.

Horse-riding is non-U against U *riding*. From the non-U point of view the expression is reasonable, for to the non-U there are other kinds of riding (cf. non-U *to go for a motor-ride* / U *to go for a drive in a motor-car*). But *bicycle-ride* is normal.

Ill in *I was very ill on the boat* is non-U against U *sick*.

Jack. At cards, *jack* is non-U against U *knave*, save in *jackpot* (at poker). My son, A. W. P. Ross, kindly calls my attention to the following passage from *Great Expectations* (ed. of 1861, vol. I, p. 126): " 'He calls the knaves, Jacks, this boy!' said Estella with disdain."

La-di-da is an expression with which the non-U stigmatise a U habit, speech-habit, or person.

Lounge is a name given by the non-U to a room in their houses; for U-speakers, *hall* or *dining-room* might well be the nearest equivalent (but all speakers, of course, speak of the *lounge* of a hotel).

non-U *mental* / U *mad.*

A *matter of business* is non-U (as in *Say you've come to see him on a matter of business*).

Mention: If you don't mind my mentioning it is non-U.

Mirror (save in compounds such as *driving-*, *shaving-mirror*) is non-U against U *looking-glass.*

non-U *note-paper* / U *writing-paper.*[22]

Pardon! is used by the non-U in three main ways: (1) if the hearer does not hear the speaker properly; (2) as an apology (e.g. on brushing by someone in a passage); (3) after hiccupping or belching. The normal U-correspondences are very curt, viz. (1) *What?* (2) *Sorry!* (3) [Silence], though, in the first two cases, U-parents and

---

[22] This distinction (as well as some others, e.g. non-U *perfume* / U *scent*) is noted by Miss Nancy Mitford, *The Pursuit of Love* (1945 ed., p. 31).

U-governesses are always trying to make children say something "politer"—*What did you say?* and *I'm frightfully sorry* are certainly possible. For Case 3 there are other non-U possibilities, e.g. *Manners! Beg Pardon! Pardon me!*

To Pass a (nasty) remark. He passed the remark that . . . is non-U.

Pleased to meet you! This is a very frequent non-U response to the greeting *How d'you do?* U-speakers normally just repeat the greeting; to reply to the greeting (e.g. with *Quite well, thank you*) is non-U.

Posh "smart" is essentially non-U but, recently, it has gained ground among schoolboys of all classes.

non-U *preserve* / U *jam*.

non-U *radio* / U *wireless* (but *radio* technically as in aircraft).

Rude meaning "indecent" is non-U; there is no universal U-correspondent.

non-U *serviette* / U *table-napkin*; perhaps the best known of all the linguistic class-indicators of English.

Study in *He's studying for an exam.* is definitely non-U (U: *working for*).

Teacher is essentially non-U, though *school-teacher* is used by the U to indicate a non-U teacher. The U equivalent is *master, mistress* with prefixed attribute (as *maths-mistress*). Non-U children often refer to their teachers without article (as, *Teacher says* . . .).

non-U *toilet-paper* / U *lavatory-paper*.

non-U *wealthy* / U *rich*.

Before concluding with some general remarks, there are two points which may appropriately receive mention here.

First, *slang*. There seems no doubt that, in the nineties and at least up to 1914, U-speakers (particularly young ones) were rather addicted to slang. Today, however, U-speakers use it little and regard much use of it as non-U—save, of course, in special circumstances (e.g. in the case of young boys at school). American slang is especially deprecated (save, perhaps, for *O.K.*). The ultimate War, like the penultimate one, brought a flood of slang into the Services, some of it a very vivid kind as, for instance, R.A.F. slang *He tore me off a strip* meaning "he reprimanded me severely," *I was shot down in flames* meaning "I was completely overwhelmed in the argument." Since the War, there has been an unfortunate tendency for non-Service personnel to use Service slang and it is clear that Service personnel regard such use as in very poor taste. Nevertheless, the expressions *I've had it!* (meaning, essentially, "I have *not* had it") and *That's a bad show*, have become very frequent among all classes of speakers.

Secondly, *changing one's voice*.[23] In England today—just as much as in the England of many years ago—the question "Can a non-U speaker become a U-speaker?"[24] is one noticeably of paramount importance for many Englishmen (and for some of their wives). The answer is that an adult can never attain complete success. Moreover, it must be remembered that, in these matters, U-speakers have ears to hear, so that one single pronunciation, word, or phrase will suffice to brand an apparent

[23] This phrase is my own coinage (of many years ago); I know of no other expression.

[24] Logically, the converse question "Can a U-speaker become a non-U-speaker?" should also arise, but, in practice, it seems not to—even the staunchest of inverted snobs apparently draws the line here. At all events I have only come across one case of it (in Leeds).

U-speaker as originally non-U (for U-speakers themselves never make "mistakes"). Under these circumstances, efforts to change voice are surely better abandoned. But, in fact, they continue in full force and in all
strata of society. On the whole, the effect is deleterious.
Thus, to take only one example: in village schools, any
natural dialect that is still left to the children will have
superimposed upon it the language of the primary
school-teacher (a class of people entirely non-U) so that
the children leave school speaking a mixture which has
nothing to recommend it. In concluding this paragraph,
I may mention that there is one method of effecting
change of voice, provided the speaker is young enough.
This is, to send him[25] first to a preparatory school, then
to a good public-school. This method is one that has been
approved for more than a century and, at the moment, it
is almost completely effective. It is interesting to speculate upon the state of affairs which will arise when the
day comes when virtually no U-speaker will be able to
afford to educate his children at these kinds of schools
(this day has already dawned).

If we consider the wider implications of the linguistic
class-indication discussed above, two points immediately
arise: the linguistic class-indicators are almost all philo-
logically trivial and, apparently, almost all of a very
ephemeral nature. I am convinced that a thorough historical study of the class-indicators discussed above
would reveal many present-day U-features as non-U at
an earlier period and vice versa. To take an example. In
his *Critical pronouncing dictionary and expositor of the
English language*, published in 1791, J. Walker is clearly

[25] Today similar arrangements can be made for girls; the older
approved method was, of course, a U-governess.

trying to differentiate between U and non-U usage. Yet nearly all the points mentioned by him—only one hundred and sixty years ago—are now "dead" and without class-significance, in that one of the pronunciations given is today no longer known in any kind of English save dialect. Only one of Walker's U indicators (*in'* of *huntin'*, *shootin'*, and *fishin'*) is so recognised by me and even that one I regard as belonging to an era earlier than my own. In two cases of double pronunciations, today's U alternative is chosen by Walker as the non-U one, viz. (I quote) (1) "*Either* and *neither* are . . . often pronounced *eye-ther* and *nigh-ther*. . . . Analogy, however, without hesitation, gives the diphthong the sound of long *e* and rhymes them with *breather*, one who breathes. This is the pronunciation Mr. Garrick always gave to these words, and which is undoubtedly the true one." (2) "The proper names *Derby* and *Berkeley*, still retain the old sound, as if written *Darby* and *Barkeley*: but even these, in polite usage, are getting into the common sound, nearly as if written *Durby* and *Burkeley*." Walker feels strongly on various matters: "The vulgar . . . pronounce the *o* obscurely, and sometimes as if followed by *r*, as *winder*, *feller*, for *window* and *fellow*; but this is almost too despicable for notice"—but the pronunciation of *fellow* fulminated against by Walker is, to me, old-fashioned U (though I make the word rhyme with *bellow* myself).

Among European languages, English is, surely, the one most suited to the study of linguistic class-distinction. I do not really know how far such a thing may exist in others. In Finnish, I have the impression that no phenomena of the sort exist. In German, there may well have been something comparable; certainly, I recall that, in good Potsdam society of the late twenties, the expression *küss' die hand* (on introduction to a female) was definitely frowned on—but this society has vanished without trace. In present-day Russian, the distinction between the two plurals of *ofitser* "officer"—*ofitsery* and *ofitsera*—is certainly one of class. There seems to be remarkably little literature on the subject save perhaps (rather naturally) by Russians and/or as concerns Russian. The position in Russia is indeed interesting, for, in that country, it is obviously desirable to speak in a non-U manner rather than in a U one. (There is an excellent book on the subject, in Russian, by Zhirmunskii.) It is to be hoped that more studies of linguistic class-distinction in the European languages will one day be forthcoming.

However, the general concept of a certain variant of a language appertaining to a certain section of its speakers (e.g. old women, or children) is one very well-known to anthropologists and it is, no doubt, in the African jungle and among the Red Indians that we shall find the generalised form of the linguistic indicators of our English class-distinction. This is a suitable point at which to end this article, for we have now reached that awkward terrain where Linguistics marches with Anthropology—and the anthropologists have, alas, not been appreciably active here.

A SELECTED BIBLIOGRAPHY

The writers whose names are starred are represented in this anthology.

*Beardsley, Monroe C. *See* Wimsatt and Beardsley.

*Becker, Alton L. *See also* Christensen, Becker, *et al.*

——. "A Tagmemic Approach to Paragraph Analysis." *College Composition and Communication*, XVI (1965), 237-242.

*Booth, Wayne C. *The Rhetoric of Fiction.* Chicago, 1961.

——. "The Rhetorical Stance." *College Composition and Communication*, XIV (1963), 139-145.

*Burke, Kenneth. *A Grammar of Motives.* New York, 1945.

——. *A Rhetoric of Motives.* New York, 1950.

——. *The Rhetoric of Religion.* Boston, 1961.

*Christensen, Francis. *See also* Christensen, Becker, *et al.*

——. "A Generative Rhetoric of the Sentence." *College Composition and Communication*, XIV (1963), 155-161.

——. "Notes Toward a New Rhetoric." *College English*, XXV (1963), 7-18.

Christensen, Francis; Alton L. Becker; Paul C. Rodgers, Jr.; Josephine Miles; and David H. Karrfalt. "Symposium on the Paragraph." *College Composition and Communication*, XVII (1966), 60-87.

Flesch, Rudolf F. *The Art of Readable Writing.* New York, 1949.

Gilkinson, Howard; Stanley F. Paulson; and Donald E. Sikkink. "Effects of Order and Authority in an Argumentative Speech." *Quarterly Journal of Speech*, XL (1954), 183-192.

Graves, Robert, and Alan Hodge. *Reader over Your Shoulder.* New York, 1943.

Harris, Zellig S. "Discourse Analysis." *Language*, XXVIII (1952), 1-30.

Holloway, John. *The Victorian Sage: Studies in Argument.* London, 1953.

*Hovland, Carl I., *et al. The Order of Presentation in Persuasion.* New Haven, 1957.

Karrfalt, David H. *See* Christensen, Becker, *et al.*

Miles, Josephine. *See* Christensen, Becker, *et al.*

*Milic, Louis T. "Theories of Style and Their Implications for the Teaching of Composition." *College Composition and Communication,* XVI (1965), 66-69.

Natanson, Maurice, and Henry W. Johnstone, Jr. *Philosophy, Rhetoric, and Argumentation.* University Park, Pa., 1965.

Nebergall, Roger E., ed. *Dimensions of Rhetorical Scholarship.* Norman, Okla., 1963.

*Ohmann, Richard. "In lieu of a New Rhetoric." *College English,* XXVI (1964), 17-22.

———. "Literature as Sentences." *College English,* XXVII (1966), 261-267.

———. *Shaw: The Style and the Man.* Middletown, Conn., 1962.

Parker, John P. "Some Organizational Variables and Their Effect upon Comprehension." *Journal of Communication,* XII (1962), 27-32.

Pike, Kenneth L. "Beyond the Sentence." *College Composition and Communication,* XV (1964), 129-135.

Rodgers, Paul C. Jr. *See also* Christensen, Becker, *et al.*

———. "A Discourse-centered Rhetoric of the Paragraph." *College Composition and Communication,* XVII (1966), 2-11.

Schwartz, Joseph, and John A. Rycenga, eds. *The Province of Rhetoric.* New York, 1965.

Sebeok, Thomas A., ed. *Style in Language.* Cambridge, Mass., 1960.

*Sledd, James. "Applied Grammar: Some Notes on English Prose Style." *A Short Introduction to English Grammar.* Chicago, 1959. Pp. 259-334.

*Steinmann, Martin Jr. "Freshman English: A Hypothesis and a Proposal." *Journal of Higher Education,* XXXVII (1966), 24-32.

———. "The Old Novel and the New." In *From Jane Austen to Joseph Conrad.* Ed. Robert C. Rathburn and Martin Steinmann, Jr. Minneapolis, 1958. Pp. 286-306.

*Stevenson, Charles L. *Ethics and Language.* New Haven, 1944.

Stoll, Elmer Edgar. *From Shakespeare to Joyce.* Garden City, 1944.

Waldock, A. J. A. *Paradise Lost and Its Critics.* Cambridge, Eng., 1947.

Wimsatt, W. K. Jr., and Monroe C. Beardsley. "The Affective Fallacy." *The Verbal Icon: Studies in the Meaning of Poetry* (1954). Paperback ed. New York, 1958. Pp. 21-39.